The Enigma (........aku And Puma Punku: A Visitor's Guide

Copyright Brien Foerster 2015

Seemingly machined "H blocks" found in relative abundance at Puma Punku

Dedication

How such an out of the way cluster of ancient and heavily damaged stone structures can attract so much attention intrigues me. Tiwanaku and Puma Punku sit, almost brooding on the high Altiplano of Bolivia, just half an hour from the Peruvian border and a 5-minute drive from a major highway. Yet their mere presence confounds the brightest of intellects, and is the bane of many archaeologists who try to explain the amazing and precise flat and compound stone surfaces as being the works of people wearing loincloths and having only bronze chisels and stone hammers as tools.

My thanks to the great minds that shaped the blocks with such intricate detail presumably thousands of years ago, and to those who have accompanied me in the present in exploring them. The list of the latter includes the brilliant engineer Christopher Dunn, authors David Hatcher Childress and Hugh Newman, as well as geologist Dr. Robert Schoch. And to my dear Irene; who is as intrigued as I am...

Chapters

1/ Introduction

An enigma is a thing, place or situation that makes the mind ponder, often for extended periods of time, about its origin, purpose, who or what was involved in it, and sometimes all three and more. Such are the subjects of this book. When one has at least a small amount of knowledge pertaining to the megalithic wonders of the ancient world, South America in particular and Peru and Bolivia specifically, Tiwanaku is usually on the list of the top mysterious places, but living deep in the shadows behind the famous "lost city of the Inca" Machu Picchu.

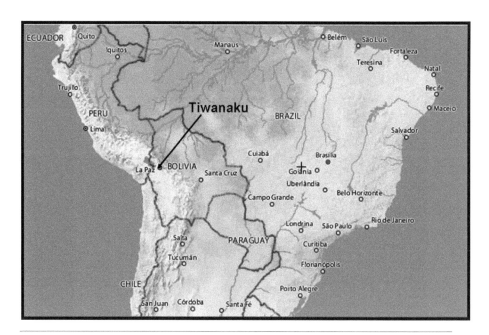

Location of Tiwanaku and Puma Punku

Located near the south shore of Lake Titicaca, the highest navigable body of water on the planet, and chilled by the high Altiplano winds, Tiwanaku sits as a barren outpost of some seemingly lost culture, abandoned by its original builders, and then adopted by others.

Detail of the location of Tiwanaku, also written Tiahuanaco

According to most people's modern day guide to knowledge, via the internet; Wikipedia; Tiwanaku (Spanish: Tiahuanaco and Tiahuanacu) is an important Pre-Columbian archaeological site in western Bolivia, South America. Tiwanaku is recognized by Andean scholars as one of the most important precursors to the Inca Empire, flourishing as the ritual and administrative capital of a major state power for approximately five hundred years. The ruins of the ancient city state are near the south-eastern shore of Lake Titicaca in the La Paz Department, Ingavi Province, Tiwanaku 6The site was first recorded in written history by Spanish conquistador and self-acclaimed "first chronicler of the Indies" Pedro Cieza de León. Leon stumbled upon the remains of Tiwanaku in 1549 while searching for the Inca capital Qullasuyu. Some have hypothesized that Tiwanaku's modern name is related to the Aymara term *taypiqala*, meaning "stone in the center", alluding to the belief that it lay at the center of the world. However, the name by which Tiwanaku was known to its inhabitants may have been lost, as the people of Tiwanaku had no written language.

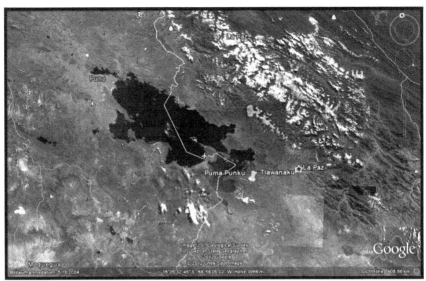
Satellite map of Tiwanaku and Puma Punku's location

"Stone in the Center" most likely refers to the place being the capital/center of a given cultural area, rather than the center of the world as a whole. This would be very similar to the Inca, the supposed offshoot of the Tiwanaku culture, who called their capital, Cuzco (or Cusco or even Qosqo) as the "Navel of the World." The Inca were of course referring to the center of "their world."

And of Puma Punku: again, according to Wikipedia, Pumapunku, also called "Puma Punku" or "Puma Puncu", is part of a large temple complex or monument group that is part of the Tiwanaku Site near Tiwanaku, Bolivia. In Aymara, its name means, "The Door of the Cougar". The Pumapunku complex consists of an unwalled western court, a central unwalled esplanade, a terraced platform mound that is faced with megalithic stone, and a walled eastern court. The Pumapunku is a terraced earthen mound that is faced with megalithic blocks. It is 167.36 m wide along its north-south axis and 116.7 m long along its east-west axis. On the northeast and southeast corners of the Pumapunku it has 20-meter wide projections that extend 27.6 meters north and south from the rectangular mound. The eastern edge of the Pumapunku is occupied by what is called the "Plataforma Lítica." The Plataforma Lítica consists of a stone terrace that is 6.75 by 38.72 meters in dimension. This terrace is paved with multiple enormous stone blocks. The Plataforma Lítica contains the largest stone slab found in both the Pumapunku and Tiwanaku Site. This stone slab is 7.81 meters long, 5.17 meters wide and averages 1.07 meters thick. Based upon the specific gravity of the red sandstone from which it was carved, this stone slab has been estimated to weigh 131 metric tons.

The three major questions about both Tiwanaku and Puma Punku are, clearly; when were they built, who built them, and how was the stone shaped? The latter is the most perplexing of all, because the precision of some of the stones, especially those of grey diorite, which is a hard igneous rock, as hard or more so than granite, supposedly coming from a source near Copacabana which is approximately 90 km away.

What clearly seems to be an engineered andesite or diorite stone at Puma Punku

The main reason why both Tiwanaku and Puma Punku are enigmas is that, for one thing, the people who live there now, the Aymara, have only been in the area for probably 1000 or so years, driving out the Inca, who were earlier inhabitants. Or, it is probably more correct to say the proto-Inca, because it is believed that the first true Inca, Manco Capac and his sister/wife Mama Occllo, were forced to leave the area as the result of a 40-year drought.

This fact, coupled with the somewhat worn out statement that "they had no written form of language" contributes to the fact that so little is known of either of these sites, and I do say either, because even a cursory inspection shows that they were not contemporary settlements. The one factor is the difference in stone used, and the level of craftsmanship, but the latter we will get to later. Some people are under the false assumption that Tiwanaku was built by the Inca; far from it. An excerpt from Graham Hancock's watershed masterpiece, "Fingerprints of the Gods" clues us in on this. Of the few early chronicles written by Native people soon after the conquest by the Spanish, beginning in 1532, the works of Garcilaso de la Vega stand out. His mother was a full blood royal Inca, and his father Spanish. In his great book "Royal Commentaries of the Inca," still available, in English and in paperback, he recounts what Tiwanaku (and presumably Puma Punku) looked like when viewed by someone 400 years ago:

We must now say something about the large and almost incredible buildings of Tiahuanaco. There is an artificial hill, of great height, built on stone foundations so that the earth will not slide. There are gigantic figures carved in stone ... these are much worn which shows their great antiquity. There are walls, the stones of which are so enormous it is difficult to imagine what human force could have put them in place. And there are the remains of strange buildings, the most remarkable being stone portals, hewn out of solid rock; these stand on bases anything up to 30 feet long, 15 feet wide and 6 feet thick, base and portal being all of one piece ... How, and with the use of what tools or implements, massive works of such size could be achieved are questions which we are unable to answer ... Nor can it be imagined how such enormous stones could have been brought here ...

And Pedro Cieza de Leon, another early chronicler, of Spanish blood, who was an early visitor to Tiwanaku:

'I asked the natives whether these edifices were built in the time of the Inca,' wrote the chronicler Pedro Cieza de Leon, 'They laughed at the question, affirming that they were made long before the Inca reign and ... that they had heard from their forebears that everything to be seen there appeared suddenly in the course of a single night ...'

Presumably no looting of the stones of the sights had occurred to any great degree at this time, so both of these early writers were able to see Tiwanaku and Puma Punku more or less in their undisturbed "time capsule" state.

The stone used at Tiwanaku, at least the original structures, which were the large pillar-like obelisks, is andesite, while Puma Punku is a grey andesite and red sandstone. The two sites are right next to each, and so many people regard them as being contemporary. However, the major difference in quality of workmanship most likely negates this idea. And why would mine be a preposterous notion? Many cities in Europe for example, Athens and Rome being classic examples, have the remains of buildings which date back at least 2000 years living in close proximity with ones made last year. Of course, in these cases the differences in building materials is obvious.

The Pantheon in Rome, Italy

The Pantheon, or at least the latest version of it, was completed supposedly about 126 AD; an earlier version of it had supposedly burned. But what makes this photo interesting is that here it sits with renaissance buildings right next to it; and shows that just because buildings are in close proximity to each other, does not mean they are of a contemporary age.

And so it would seem with Tiwanaku and Puma Punku. According to the conventional archaeological story, the area around Tiwanaku may have been inhabited as early as 1500 BC as a small agriculturally based village. (1) Most research, though, is based around the Tiwanaku IV and V periods between AD 300 and AD 1000, during which Tiwanaku grew significantly in power. During the time period between 300 BC and AD 300 Tiwanaku is thought to have been a moral and cosmological center to which many people made pilgrimages. The ideas of cosmological prestige are the precursors to Tiwanaku's powerful empire. (2)

As for Puma Punku, a radiocarbon date was obtained from the lowermost and oldest layer of mound fill. This layer was deposited during the first of three construction epochs and dates the initial construction of the Puma Punku at 1510 ±25 B.P. C14 (AD 440; calibrated, AD 536–600). Since the radiocarbon date came from the lowermost and oldest layer of mound fill underlying the diorite and sandstone stonework, the stonework must have been constructed sometime after 1510 ±25 B.P. C14. The excavation trenches of Vranich show that the clay, sand, and gravel fill of the Puma Punku complex lies directly on the sterile middle Pleistocene sediments. These excavation trenches also demonstrated the lack of any so called pre-Andean Middle Horizon cultural deposits within the area of the Tiwanaku Site adjacent to the Puma Punku complex. (3)

How much of Tiwanaku and Puma Punku looked during early excavations

Tiwanaku's location between the lake and dry highlands provided key resources of fish, wild birds, plants, and herding grounds for camelid, particularly llamas. The Titicaca Basin is the most productive environment in the area with predictable and abundant rainfall, which the Tiwanaku culture learned to harness and use in their farming. As one goes further east, the Altiplano is an area of very dry arid land. The high altitude Titicaca Basin required the development of a distinctive farming technique known as "flooded-raised field" agriculture (*suka kollus*). They comprised a significant percentage of the agriculture in the region, along with irrigated fields, pasture, terraced fields and qochas (artificial ponds) farming. Artificially raised planting mounds are separated by shallow canals filled with water. The canals supply moisture for growing crops, but they also absorb heat from solar radiation during the day. This heat is gradually emitted during the bitterly cold nights that often produce frost, endemic to the region, providing thermal insulation. (4)

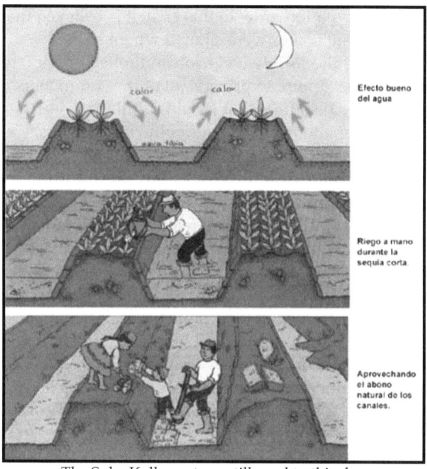

The Suka Kollu system, still used to this day

The above description is also thought to have included Puma Punku. So the dating of both sites, regarded by many as a single one, begins, in the conventional sense, about 1500 BC. But what the academics fail to answer, or seemingly even take into account, are the amazing levels of stone shaping prowess found at Tiwanaku, but even more so at Puma Punku. This we shall delve into later.

As the population grew in this area, it is believed that occupational niches were created where each member of the society had a job and relied on the elites of the empire to provide all of the commoners with all the resources that would fulfill their needs. Some occupations include agriculturists, herders, pastoralists, etc. Along with this separation of occupations, there was also a hierarchal stratification within the empire. The elites of Tiwanaku lived inside four walls that were surrounded by a moat, supposedly. This moat, some believe, was to create the image of a sacred island. Inside the walls there were many images of human origin that only the elites were privileged to, despite the fact that images represent the beginning of all humans not only the elite. Commoners may have only ever entered this structure for ceremonial purposes since it was home to the holiest of shrines. (5)

Layout of the Tiwanaku and Puma Punku complex

It is theorized the Pumapunku complex as well as its surrounding temples of Tiwanaku, the Akapana pyramid, Kalasasaya, Putuni and Kerikala functioned as spiritual and ritual centers for the Tiwanaku people. This area might have been viewed as the center of the Andean world, attracting pilgrims from far away to marvel in its beauty. These structures transformed the local landscape; Pumapunku was purposely integrated with Illimani Mountain, a sacred peak that the Tiwanaku possibly believed to be home to the spirits of their dead. This area was believed to have existed between heaven and Earth. The spiritual significance and the sense of wonder would have been amplified into a "mind-altering and life-changing experience." (6)

OK; but all of this is hypothetical. The last of the Tiwanaku culture is believed to have been the beginnings of the Inca, about 1000 years ago, replaced by the Aymara people, who populate the area to this day.

The so called city and its inhabitants left no written history, and modern local people know little about the city and its activities. An archaeologically based theory asserts that around AD 400, Tiwanaku went from being a locally dominant force to a predatory state. Tiwanaku expanded its reaches into the Yungas and brought its culture and way of life to many other cultures in Peru, Bolivia, and Chile. However, Tiwanaku was not exclusively a violent culture. In order to expand its reach, it used politics to create colonies, negotiate trade agreements, and establish so-called state cults. (7)

Force was rarely necessary for the empire to expand, but on the northern end of the Basin resistance was present. There is evidence that bases of some statues were taken from other cultures and carried all the way back to the capital city of Tiwanaku where the stones were placed in a subordinate position to the Gods of the Tiwanaku in order to display the power Tiwanaku held over many. (8)

One of these could very well have been Pucara, located to the north on the Altiplano of present day Peru, at 3910m altitude, 61 km north of Juliaca, which is at the northern edge of Lake Titicaca. The story of culture Pucara dates back to 500 BC C., with the main background to the cultures Chiripa Qaluyo north and south of the lake, and so existed in full flourish long before the apex of Tiwanaku.

Sculpture garden of artefacts near the ancient site of Pucara

The community grew to urban proportions between 600 and 800 AD, becoming an important regional power in the southern Andes. According to early estimates, at its maximum extent, the city covered approximately 6.5 square kilometers, and had between 15,000–30,000 inhabitants. However, satellite imaging was used recently to map the extent of fossilized suka kollus across the three primary valleys of Tiwanaku, arriving at population-carrying capacity estimates of anywhere between 285,000 and 1,482,000 people. (9) This is lost to most visitors today, since the only structures left of any significance are the stone temple constructions. However, what is important to note is that the common people would have constructed their dwellings out of the alluvial clay/mud deposits of the area, essentially adobe mud bricks. The roofs would have been a straw thatch. Both the adobe and thatch still make up the majority of poor farmers' houses today, the odd one having corrugated metal or ceramic tile roofs.

Typical Bolivian houses of the area either under construction or abandoned

Over the years, once abandoned during the 40-year drought of the 10th century, the natural grass roofing would have given way due to solar and especially rain deterioration, and then the adobe would essentially dissolve back into the stratum. That is why very little of what could have been a city of 1,000,000 or more inhabitants now looks like a lonely cluster of stone ruins.

However, getting back to Tiwanaku when it was in its prime, it gained its power through the trade it implemented between all of the cities within its empire. The elites gained their status by control of the surplus of food obtained from all regions and redistributed among all the people. Control of llama herds became very significant to Tiwanaku, as they were essential for carrying goods back and forth between the center and the periphery. (10) The animals may also have symbolized the distance between the commoners and the elites, in that the elite clearly owned more!

The elites' power continued to grow along with the surplus of resources until about 950. At this time a dramatic shift in climate occurred, as has been discussed, which is typical for the region. A significant drop in precipitation occurred in the Titicaca Basin, with some archaeologists venturing to suggest a great drought occurred. As the rain became less and less many of the cities furthest away from Lake Titicaca began to produce fewer crops to give to the elites. As the surplus of food dropped, the elites' power began to fall. This is of course assuming that the so called elites were oligarchs, which is more of a European construct than that of a Native American one. However, it is typical of academics, especially those that are western trained, to impose their ideas of social structure on those of other cultures. The same is very true as regards the later Inca civilization, dubbed an empire by many scholars. It was in fact a confederation of states. This is covered in great detail in my two books: "A Brief History of the Incas: From Rise,

Through Reign to Ruin," and "The Inca; Before The Conquest." Both are available as e-books and paper backs from www.hiddenincatours.com as well as through www.amazon.com.

Due to the resiliency of the raised fields, the capital city became the last place of production, but in the end even the intelligent design of the fields was no match for the weather. Tiwanaku disappeared around 1000 because food production, the empire's source of power and authority, dried up. The land was not inhabited again for many years and then so by the Aymara people, which we have already discussed.

Beyond the northern frontier of the Tiwanaku state a new power started to emerge in the beginning of the 13th century, the Inca Empire. In 1445 Pachacutec Inca Yupanqui (the ninth Inca) absorbed the Titicaca regions. He incorporated and developed what was left from the Tiwanaku patterns of culture, and the Inca officials were superimposed upon the existing local officials. Quechua was made the official language and sun worship the official religion. So, the last traces of the Tiwanaku civilization were integrated or deleted. This then ends a cursory overview of the site(s) and a cursory exploration of the culture(s) thought to have dwelt there. We now move on to architecture and art.

Drawing of the Inca Pachacutec

2/ Tiwanaku Architecture and Art

In this discussion, Tiwanaku and Puma Punku are usually discussed together, and so we shall do so here. Later on, we can talk about possible differences. Tiwanaku and Puma Punku monumental architecture is characterized by large stones of exceptional workmanship, especially at Puma Punku. In contrast to the masonry style of the later Inca, Tiwanaku stone architecture usually employs rectangular ashlar blocks laid in regular courses, and monumental structures were frequently fitted with elaborate drainage systems. This is curious, because the true works of the Inca are in fact far inferior to that of their proposed Tiwanaku ancestors. The Inca are now believed to have been the engineers and builders of the agricultural terraces, called Andene, that are still found in the Sacred Valley and around Cuzco, but not the megalithic structures, such as Sachsayhuaman and the Coricancha in Cuzco. They were the builders of most of Machu Picchu, during the reign of the Sapa (high) Inca Pachacutec in the 15th century, but the more exacting masonry seems in fact to belong to an earlier culture, and perhaps two. All of this is covered in my e-books " Inca Footprints: Walking Tours Of Cusco And The Sacred Valley Of Peru" and "Machu Picchu: Virtual Guide And Secrets Revealed" which are available at www.hiddenincatours.com and www.amazon.com.

Sketch from the 19th century of one Puma Punku sandstone block

The drainage systems of the Akapana and Puma Punku include conduits composed of red sandstone blocks held together by ternary (copper/arsenic/nickel) bronze architectural clamps. The I-shaped architectural clamps of the Akapana were created by cold hammering of ingots. In contrast, the clamps of the Puma Punku were created by pouring molten metal into I-shaped sockets. (11) This would indicate that either two distinct techniques were at use at the same time, or that one preceded the other.

The cold hammering and shaping of the clamps is not however restricted to the Akapana, as the above reference suggests. Many of the recesses in the massive red sandstone foundation blocks at Puma Punku, which vary in size from about a foot long to, more than 2 feet, also employed this technique. The shaping of cold and hard metal is indeed a challenge, but nothing in comparison to the smelting of molten metal, which would require a smelting operation on site. Melting a complex amalgam of metals at such a high altitude would most likely have been way beyond the capability of a primitive culture.

Another term which describes these recessed cuts in the stone is "key stone" and has been used a lot by such researchers as David Hatcher Childress, who accompanied me and Hugh Newman in November of 2011 for the filming of an episode of the Ancient Aliens television series. These features are not exclusive to this particular geographic location, but can also be seen in Cusco, Ollantaytambo in Peru's Sacred Valley, Egypt, Angkor Wat in Cambodia and other places that have megalithic structures.

Recesses where metal clamps were used on massive red sandstone slabs

A rounded "key stone" cut which would have required a molten clamp

Example of the drainage system at Tiwanaku

The main architectural appeal of the site comes from the carved images and designs on some of these blocks, carved doorways, and giant stone monoliths. (12) This is especially true at Puma Punku, where there are two sun gates, similar in shape and design to the famous one now at the Tiwanaku location, which are lying flat on the ground, and are not often or easily observed. A close inspection by myself reveals that a drill of some kind seems to have been employed, and perhaps a high speed vibratory or router like tool to sculpt relief channels in the upper portions of each of these Sun Gates. More about this later.

The quarries, from which the stone blocks used in the construction of structures at Tiwanaku came, lie at significant distances from this site. The red sandstone used in this site's structures have been determined by petrographic analysis to come from a quarry 10 kilometers away—a remarkable distance considering that the largest of these stones weighs 131 metric tons. (12) The grey andesite (or some would call grey diorite) stones that were used to create the most elaborate carvings and monoliths, especially at Puma Punku originate from the Copacabana peninsula, located across Lake Titicaca, about 90 km away. One theory is that these giant andesite stones, which weigh over 40 tons were transported some 90 kilometers across Lake Titicaca on reed boats, then laboriously dragged another 10 kilometers to the city. This I find absolutely comical, and will not bother to state the reference. 40 tons is the equivalent of more than 25 average passenger automobiles; transported by totora reed boats? And then dragged another 10 kilometers? Using what as rollers? Non-existent tree trunks, or did they also fashion cylindrical stone rollers out the same material employing bronze chisels and stone hammers? How preposterous.

Even a large reed boat such as this could not carry 40 tons!

The buildings that have been excavated include the Akapana, and Puma Punku stepped platforms, the Kalasasaya and Putuni enclosures, and the Semi-Subterranean Temple. These are the structures that are visible to the modern visitor. Many theories for Tiwanaku's architecture construction have been proposed. One is that they used a luk'a which is a standard measurement of about sixty centimeters. Another argument is for the Pythagorean Ratio. This idea calls for right triangles at a ratio of five to four to three used in the gateways to measure all parts. Lastly, another theory argues that Tiwanaku had a system set for individual elements dependent on context and composition. This is shown in the construction of similar gateways ranging from diminutive to monumental size proving that scaling factors did not affect proportion. With each added element, the individual pieces shifted to fit together. However, I find the latter very hard to believe. Such precision stone work, especially at Puma Punku would require very thoughtful planning, and systematic execution based on some form of proportionality. Analysis of the structures is still clearly in its infancy, and could use the input of engineers, architects, and artisans, including contemporary stone masons and sculptors to truly solve the riddles. Leaving it to a small or even large group of archaeologists who have no real training in the previously mentioned disciplines is simply dangerous and misleading.

Throughout their reign, the Tiwanaku shared domination with the Wari. The Wari culture rose and fell around the same time and was centered 500 miles north in the southern highlands of Peru. The relationship between the two groups is unknown either being cooperative or antagonistic. Definite interaction between the two is proved by their shared iconography in art, or at least this is presumed so. Significant elements of both of these styles (the split eye, trophy heads, and staff-bearing profile figures, for example) seem to have been derived from that of the earlier Pucara culture in the northern Titicaca Basin, whom we have mentioned earlier. The Tiwanaku created a powerful ideology, using previous Andean icons that spread throughout their sphere of influence using extensive trade routes and shamanistic art. Tiwanaku art consisted of legible, outlined figures depicted in curvilinear style with a naturalistic manner, while Wari art used the same symbols in a more abstract, rectilinear style with a militaristic manner. (13) This suggests an influence, but clearly does not prove it.

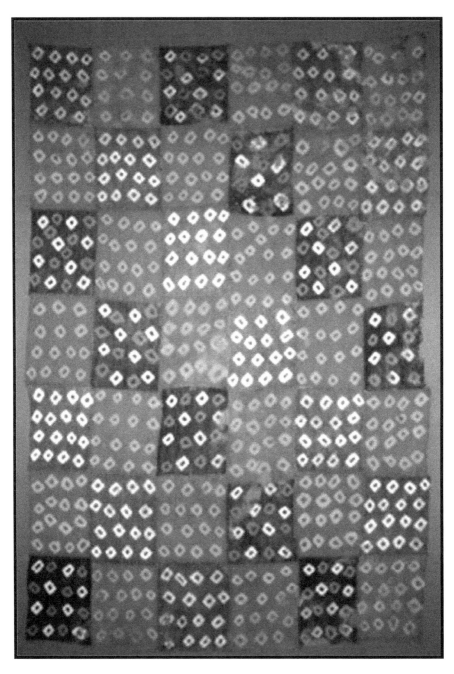

Example of a Wari, or Huari culture textile

Tiwanaku sculpture is comprised typically of blocky column-like figures with huge, flat square eyes, and detailed with shallow relief carving. Again, it is at Puma Punku, and those sculptures which were moved from Puma Punku to their present homes at Tiwanaku and its new museum, as well as those on display in La Paz, which have this appearance. The red sandstone monolithic sculptures appear to be much cruder in form, and I believe were made later, after the fall of the higher cultures that built the enigmatic masterpiece monuments of Tiwanaku, and especially Puma Punku.

Classic andesite or diorite sculpture

They are often holding ritual objects like the Ponce Stela or the Bennett Monolith. Some have been found holding severed heads such as the figure on the Akapana, possibly a puma-shaman. These images suggest ritual human beheading, which correlate with the discovery of headless skeletons found under the Akapana. This however, is also a subject of much debate.

A cruder and possibly later red sandstone sculpture

David Hatcher Childress next to one of the more refined red sandstone sculptures

Ceramics and textiles were also present in their art, composed of bright colours and stepped patterns. An important ceramic artefact is the kero, a drinking cup that was ritually smashed after ceremonies and placed in burials. However, as the empire expanded, ceramics changed in the society. The earliest ceramics were "coarsely polished, deeply incised brown ware and a burnished polychrome incised ware". Later the so called Qeya style became popular "Typified by vessels of a soft, light brown ceramic paste". These ceramics included libation bowls and bulbous bottom vases. (14)

Classic ceramic vessels believed to be of the Tiwanaku people

Examples of textiles are tapestries and tunics. The objects typically depicted herders, effigies, trophy heads, sacrificial victims, and felines. The key to spreading religion and influence from the main site to the satellite centers was through small portable objects that held ritual religious meaning. They were created in wood, engraved bone, and cloth and depicted puma and jaguar effigies, incense burners, carved wooden hallucinogenic snuff tablets, and human portrait vessels. Like the Moche, Tiwanaku portraits had individual characteristics in them. (15)

Now we move on to the religious/spiritual beliefs that the people of Tiwanaku, and possibly Puma Punku practiced.

3/ Religious/Spiritual Beliefs

As these people had no written language, though, like their descendants, the Inca, they may have had a hieroglyphic system which has not been fully decoded, what is known of their religious beliefs are based on archaeological interpretation and some myths, which may have been passed down to the Incas and the Spanish. They seem to have worshipped many gods, perhaps centered on agriculture; however, this is such a vague notion, and seemingly the best that archaeologists and anthropologists can come up with presently. One of the most important gods, in fact most probably the principal deity was Viracocha, the god of action, shaper of many worlds, and destroyer of many worlds. He created people, with two servants, namely the first Inca, Manco Capac and Mama Occlo on a great piece of rock. Then he drew sections on the rock and sent his servants to name the tribes in those areas. In Tiwanaku he created the people out of rock and brought life to them through the earth. The Tiwanaku believed that Viracocha created giants to move the massive stones that comprise much of their archaeology, but then grew unhappy with the giants and created a flood to destroy them.

Massive andesite sculpture of Viracocha in the Tiwanaku Museum

Depiction of Viracocha from the famous Gateway of the Sun

The above statement, although there is no specific reference for it, hints at the idea that the Tiwanakan people themselves admit that they were not responsible for the construction of the megaliths. If they are referring to giants, then they are hardly referring to themselves.

Other evidence, however, points to a system of ancestor worship at Tiwanaku. The preservation, use, and reconfiguration of mummy bundles and skeletal remains, like the later Inca, may suggest that this is the case. Later cultures within the area made use of large "above ground burial chambers for the social elite known as "Chullpas". These are especially the case at Sillustani, west of the city of Puno on the Peruvian side of Lake Titicaca. Similar, though smaller, structures were found within the site of Tiwanaku. (16) Kolata, as just referenced, suggests that, like the later Inca, the inhabitants of Tiwanaku may have practiced similar rituals and rites in relation to the dead. The Akapana East Building has evidence of ancestor burial. In comparison to the perceived brutal treatment of the dead on top of the Akapana, the human remains at Akapana East seem to be much less for show and more so for proper burial. The skeletons show many cut marks that were most likely made by defleshing after death.

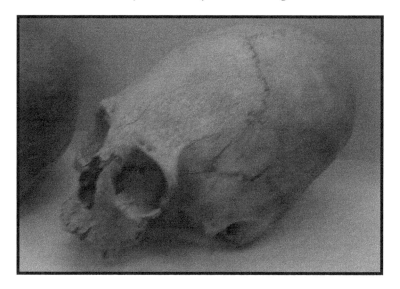

One of the intriguing elongated skulls found at Tiwanaku and Puma Punku

4/ Archaeology Of The Area

Much of the architecture of the site is in a poor state of preservation, having been subjected to looting and amateur excavations attempting to locate valuables since shortly after Tiwanaku's fall; in other words, for about a thousand years both Tiwanaku and Puma Punku have been plundered. This destruction continued during the Spanish conquest and colonial period, again mainly looking for gold and stone building materials, and during 19th century and the early 20th century, and has included quarrying stone for railroad construction and target practice by military personnel. The local church in the village of Tiwanaku is one of the best examples of the looting and "recycling" of stone. How much of these sites were moved to La Paz during colonial times and later has never been fully accounted.

Stones with holes in this Tiwanaku village church are from Puma Punku

Detail view of one of the Puma Punku blocks

Block from Puma Punku with "keystone cuts" in the Tiwanaku Village square

Another issue for archaeologists is the lack of standing buildings at the modern site. Only public, non-domestic foundations remain, with poorly reconstructed walls. The ashlar blocks used in many of these structures were mass-produced in similar styles so that they could possibly be used for multiple purposes. Throughout the period of the site certain buildings changed purposes causing a mix of artefacts that are found today. (17) This, at least, is the opinion of Jean Pierre Protzen, an American architect. It is also possible that the natural seismic upheavals and the evidence that some sort of major flooding which occurred in the distant past may have so mixed up the sediments, and re-deposited them, that the archaeologists, believing that the deeper they were digging the farther in the past they were discovering, may be untrue.

As has already been discussed, the greater population would have lived in adobe houses with natural thatching, and most likely no foundations, so there is very little if anything that remains of their existence.

Detailed study of Tiwanaku began on a small scale in the mid-nineteenth century. In the 1860s, Ephraim George Squier visited the ruins and later published maps and sketches completed during his visit. German geologist Alphons Stübel spent nine days in Tiwanaku in 1876, creating a map of the site based on careful measurements. He also made sketches and created paper impressions of carvings and other architectural features. A book containing major photographic documentation was published in 1892 by engineer B. von Grumbkow. With commentary by archaeologist Max Uhle, this was the first in-depth scientific account of the ruins.

19th century drawing of the area

Presumably the same diorite doorway seen today

Presumably how the Sun gate was seen by Squier and Stubel

Very early photos of the back side of the Sun Gate

As you can see in the above drawings and photos, Tiwanaku and Puma Punku look nothing today as they did ad recently as a century or so ago. It should be noted that the Sun Gate, or Gateway of the Sun, that now stands in the Kalasasaya, is not in its original location, having been moved sometime earlier from its original location, which is unknown. However, as we have already discussed to some degree, Puma Punku is where the majority of the grey diorite is found to this day, as well as the reconstituted walls of Tiwanaku. It is my contention that Puma Punku was exclusively composed of red sandstone as its base, and that all of the walls were of diorite, whereas the Kalasasaya and other Tiwanaku structures were andesite; a different stone altogether. It is my assumption that the Sun Gate, due to its impressive look and size, was moved to Tiwanaku from Puma Punku early on in the so-called reconstruction because there it could be seen as a show piece. The fact that it is of diorite convinces me that its original home was at Puma Punku.

The Gate of the Sun as it now looks, on a makeshift base of recycled stones

Other pieces of evidence that supports my thesis is that the fine carving and stone finishing is something that we find, again, at Puma Punku and not at Tiwanaku, and that two other Sun Gates, or at least monolithic arches very similar in proportion to the famous Gate of the Sun, as I have stated earlier, are located at Puma Punku, composed of diorite, and broken into many pieces. A further fourth one is at the top of the Akapana Pyramid, lying down and shattered, without all of the pieces present.

One of the other presumed Sun Gates at Puma Punku

One of many interpretations of what Puma Punku once looked like

In the 1960s, an attempt was made at restoring the site, but by very uninformed parties. The walls of the

Kalasasaya, are almost all reconstruction. The original stones making up the Kalasasaya would have resembled a more "Stonehenge" like style, spaced evenly apart and standing straight up. Unfortunately, the parties that made the reconstructions decided to make the Kalasasaya be enclosed by a wall that they themselves built. Ironically enough, the reconstruction itself is actually much poorer quality stonework than the people of Tiwanaku were capable of.

The saddest aspects of the above facts are that most visitors to these sites are completely unaware of what they actually may have originally looked like, and the poor contemporary assembly of the stones sheds a poor light on the original builders, who were clearly absolute masters of stone masonry art.

Drawing of the Kalasasaya prior to restoration

Photo of the Kalasasaya during excavations in the 1880s

"Reconstruction" of the Kalasasaya

Modern, academically sound archaeological excavations were performed from 1978 through the 1990s by University of Chicago anthropologist Alan Kolata and his Bolivian counterpart, Oswaldo Rivera. Among their contributions are the rediscovery of the suka kollus, accurate dating of the civilization's growth and influence, and evidence for a drought-based collapse of the Tiwanaku civilization.

Today Tiwanaku is a UNESCO world heritage site, and is administered by the Bolivian government. Recently, the Department of Archaeology of Bolivia (DINAR, directed by Javier Escalante) has been conducting excavations on the Akapana pyramid. The *Proyecto Arqueologico Pumapunku-Akapana* (PAPA, or Pumapunku-Akapana Archaeological Project) run by the University of Pennsylvania has been excavating in the area surrounding the pyramid for the past few years, and also conducting ground penetrating radar surveys of the area.

In former years, an archaeological field school offered through Harvard's Summer School Program, conducted in the residential area outside the monumental core, provoked controversy amongst local archaeologists. The program was directed by Dr. Gary Urton, (18) Harvard, expert in the quipu, which is the Inca and other culture's tabulation and accounting system made up of knotted cords, and Dr. Alexei Vranich of the University of Pennsylvania. The controversy had to do with the fact that permission to excavate Tiwanaku, being such an important site, is only provided to certified professional archaeologists and rarely to independent Bolivian scholars who scarcely can present proof of funding to carry on archaeological research. On that occasion permission was given to Harvard's Summer School to allow a team mostly composed of untrained students to dig the site. The controversy, charged with nationalistic and political undertones that characterized the archaeology of Tiwanaku faded rapidly without any response from the directors. However, the project did not continue in subsequent years.

The Kalasasaya prior to reconstruction

This is a classic example of the dilemma one has in trying to find evidence in the literature which is openly available to the public. Most of the public live with the belief that all scholarly pursuits are conducted with the highest of ethics. But the above example shows that often it is the schools with the most money and name that receive access to special sites such as Puma Punku and Tiwanaku, and not those with great intent, but lacking the degrees.

And for an independent researcher such as myself? Forget it; I would never be given access to dig. However, this hardly deters me. As you can see, by piecing the puzzle together using what is available, and exploring the sites on one's own, a fair amount of information can be gleaned.

Small clay figurine reproductions that may give insights into the original builders

We will now cover each of the major sites, one at a time, a sort of a virtual tour starting in the Tiwanaku complex. This area is enclosed within a wire fence, only open during the official hours of 9 am to 5 pm, and is composed of 5 major structures: Akapana Pyramid, Subterranean Temple, Temple of Kalasasaya, Putuni and Kerikala.

5/ Akapana Pyramid

This sign shows you what the Akapana looked like

As soon as you enter the gate, the Akapana Pyramid is on your immediate right. It is a multi-tiered structure that is mostly covered, still, with debris and soil, most likely the result of its having been abandoned and neglected for so many centuries. The Akapana is an approximately cross-shaped pyramidal structure that is 257 m wide, 197 m broad at its maximum, and 16.5 m tall. At its center, there is what appears to have been a sunken court that has been almost entirely destroyed by a deep looters excavation that extends from the center of this structure to its eastern side. Material from the looters excavation was dumped off the eastern side of the Akapana. A staircase with sculptures is present on its western side. Possible residential complexes might have occupied both the northeast and southeast corners of this structure. Originally, the Akapana was thought to have been made from a modified hill, but recent studies have shown that it is a manmade earthen mound that is faced with a mixture of large and small stone blocks. The dirt comprising Akapana appears to have been excavated from the "moat" that surrounds the site. (19)

Stairway to the top of the Akapana

The largest stone block within the Akapana, which consists of andesite, is estimated to weigh 65.70 metric tons. This is in fact a diorite Sun Gate, which, as I have previously stated, most likely came originally from Puma

Punku. The Akapana structure is proposed by archaeologists to have possibly been for the shaman-puma relationship or transformation. Tenon puma and human heads stud the upper terraces.

Partial reconstruction of the Akapana

Back side of the Akapana which appears to have been buried in mud in the past

Computer model of how the Akapana originally looked

Some researchers have speculated that the original function of the Akapana was that of a facility for processing metal ores, which are abundant the local area due to the proximity to the Andes. The large pool on top of the structure could have acted as a holding pond for water which was then channelled through the structure.

Another intriguing point is that at Tiwanaku we seem to have an interesting situation where the city's previous infrastructure was razed and completely redone just before the city was suddenly abandoned. It seems that around A.D. 700, three centuries into the existence of Tiwanaku as a monumental and powerful city, there was a sudden change to direct all construction efforts toward building what was the largest structure in the Andes. The previous monuments of the city were torn down and their stones reused to build the Akapana pyramid. The effort was too great, and the pyramid lay unfinished when the city was abandoned. One Spanish chronicler said of Tiwanaku, "They build their monuments as if their intent was never to finish them."

6/ Subterranean Temple

The Subterranean Temple as seen from the Akapana

Next to the Akapana is the Subterranean Temple; a square sunken courtyard that's unique for its north-south rather than east-west axis. The walls are covered with tenon heads of many different styles postulating that it was probably reused for different purposes over time. It was built with walls of sandstone pillars and smaller blocks of Ashlar masonry. The heads which have been imbedded in the walls are of a very poor quality, sculpturally speaking, and I get the impression that they are not original, at least most of them.

Descending into the Subterranean temple and facing the Kalasasaya

The material that the heads are made of appears to be sandstone or limestone, and of a much lighter whitish or creamy colour than the surrounding material. And again, the craftsmanship is so much poorer than especially the diorite sculptures which I presume came from Puma Punku, that they would not have been contemporary.

The poor quality of the heads and wall reconstruction

7/ Temple of Kalasasaya

Another view of the entrance to the Kalasasaya

The Kalasasaya is a large courtyard, outlined by a high gateway. It is located to the north of the Akapana and west of the Semi-Subterranean Temple. Within the courtyard is where explorers found the Gateway of the Sun, but it is contested today that this was not its original location. As we have already discussed, it seems clear that Gateway is from Puma Punku. The Kalasasaya is about 120 by 130 meters in dimension and aligned to the cardinal directions. Like the other platform mounds within Tiwanaku, it has a central sunken court. This sunken court can be reached by a monumental staircase through an opening in its eastern wall. The walls are composed of sandstone pillars that alternated with sections of smaller blocks of Ashlar masonry and incorporates tenon heads of many different styles. This wall, as it currently stands, has been reconstructed in modern times. The Kalasasaya dates back to at least 200 BCE - 200 CE. (20)

View of the outer wall of the Kalasasaya

The Kalasasaya was used as a ceremonial center and for astronomical observations, allowing users to observe and define certain astronomical activities on any date of the 365-day year. On the Fall and Spring equinoxes (21 March and 21 September, respectively, for the southern hemisphere) the light of Sun shined through the main entrance gate. This indicates that the Tiwanaku civilization understood earth/sun cycles (calendar) and astronomy well enough to incorporate them into their construction projects and activities.

Difference between the ancient standing stones and the reconstruction

Of the Putini and Kerikala not much is known, and they are actually not that interesting to look at. Both have sunken courtyards, but very little excavation has been done. Puma Punku is very intriguing however.

Andesite Viracocha sculpture inside Kalasasaya, probably originally from Puma Punku

8/ Puma Punku

As has been previously stated, Puma Punku is another man-made platform built on an east-west axis like the Akapana. It is 167.36 m wide along its north-south axis and 116.7 m broad along its east-west axis, and is 5 m tall. Identical 20-meter wide projections extend 27.6 meters north and south from the northeast and southeast corners of Puma Punku. Walled and unwalled courts and an esplanade are associated with this structure. A prominent feature of Puma Punku is a stone terrace that is 6.75 by 38.72 meters in dimension and paved of large stone blocks.

View of the Plataforma Litica red sandstone remnant

The eastern edge of Puma Punku is called the "Plataforma Lítica." The Plataforma Lítica consists of a stone terrace that is 6.75 by 38.72 meters in dimension. This terrace is paved with multiple enormous stone blocks, and contains the largest stone slab found in both the Puma Punku and Tiwanaku Site. This stone slab is 7.81 meters long, 5.17 meters wide and averages 1.07 meters thick. Based upon the specific gravity of the red sandstone from which it was carved, this stone slab has been estimated to weigh 131 metric tons. This fact on its own suggests that Puma Punku was made by engineers who were more sophisticated than those who made Tiwanaku, and the evidence of machined blocks at Puma Punku adds even further weight, because these are found, in their original location at Puma Punku and not at Tiwanaku.

The idea that Puma Punku may be an older site does not fit in well with the majority of standard academics who see human evolution, including technical evolution, as simply going from simple to more complex. However, this is what we seem to be looking at. The same case is found in Egypt, and is gaining new ground thanks to the works of independent researchers such as Graham Hancock, Robert Bauval, John Anthony West, Stephen Mehler, and the brilliant Anglo-American engineer Christopher Dunn, author of the "Giza Power Plant," a very detailed look at the clear evidence of machined granite stone works in Egypt. It is Chris' assumption, based on 20 years of careful study, that the Great Pyramid, as well as others, could very well have been a giant machine that produced electricity. The fact that it most likely, or I would say in fact clearly predates the time of the pharaohs has caused shock, dismay, and refute amongst the small clique of people we call Egyptologists.

And just as startling, but simpler in approach and yet profound in implication, is the fact that Dr. Robert Schoch, a Boston University professor, has proven beyond doubt that the erosion of the limestone body of the Sphinx in Egypt was the result of water, as in most likely rain weathering, than it was of wind borne sand. Egyptologists, in general, scoffed at the notion, stating that Egypt has not seen much in the way of rainfall for perhaps 10,000 years. This in turn sealed the deal; the Sphinx is at least 10,000 years old, and the pharaohs have not even been there for 6,000 years; someone else made it.

Puma Punku is believed to have once contained a great wharf, or so thought Arthur Posnansky, a Bolivian engineer and independent archaeologist who studied the site, as well as Tiwanaku in the 20th century, over many decades. Yet all that remains today are megalithic ruins from some cataclysmic event in history. A great earthquake? A comet that came too close to the Earth? A worldwide flood? These are all possible causes to the destruction of the once great structure that is now the ruins of Puma Punku.

Notice how jumbled the massive stones are; some still partially buried

Not only is there evidence to support the claim of a cataclysmic flood, but there is even evidence to support the theory that people once lived there before such a flood even occurred. The suspected flood could have happened somewhere around 12,000 years ago, and there is scientific evidence of tools, bones, and other material within flood alluvia, which suggests that a civilized people were there prior to any flood. Other evidence, that being carvings of bearded people that are not Andean, have been recorded throughout the area.

In general, these bearded men are regarded as being depictions of Viracocha, the creator, or of men who were themselves called Viracocha or Viracochans.

It is highly unlikely that any of the stones in Puma Punku were cut using ancient stone cutting techniques, at least not those that we are aware of. As we have already discussed, the only tools seemingly available at the time would have been stone hammers, and perhaps a bronze chisels. The fact that bronze clasps have been found at Puma Punku means that the builders clearly had knowledge of metallurgy, difficult to conduct at high altitude, since it is even hard to boil water at this height above sea level. But the accuracy and fine finish would be practically impossible to achieve using these tools; the stone is simply too hard, and the edges too crisp.

Keystone cuts at Puma Punku which held bronze clasps

The stones in Puma Punku are made up of granite, and diorite, and so many people speculate that diamond tools, and probably diamond power tools, which have to have been employed. Through discussions with Christopher Dunn, the engineer whom I have spoken of before, it seems that diamond tools do make sense or carborundum (slightly softer than diamond and used in industrial applications today. The alternative idea that Chris suggests is that vibrational tools could have been used; moving at very high speed, with carborundum or diamond encrusted cutters lubricated with water, or another liquid.

Not only were these stones cut somehow, but they were finely cut. The cuts on these stones are perfectly straight. The holes cored into these stones are perfect, and all of equal depth. How is it that these ancient people were able to cut stones like this? It is as if only master builders were allowed to come in and construct Puma Punku. All of the blocks are cut so that they interlock, and fit together like a puzzle. There is no mortar. There are only great stones that once fit together creating a structure some four levels high.

Classic example of precision cut and holes in diorite at Puma Punku

If these people could have moved these large stones to this precise location, then obviously they also had a way to place them one on top of another, but how in the world was this accomplished?

There are no trees in the area, the nearest quarry is at least 10 miles away, and we have no records as to how any of this could have been done. As far as most are concerned, there is no way that the Andean people could have done this 2500 years ago. If they couldn't have done it, how is it possible that an even older group of people accomplished it?

Bench in the Tiwanaku Museum recycled from Puma Punku; notice the drill holes

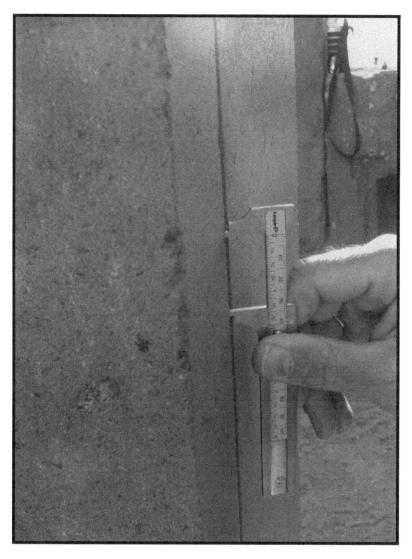

Callipers show that the spacing between many holes in this stone is uniform

9/ Arthur Posnansky: Rebel With A Cause

Posnansky with the so-called Bennett sculpture

Arthur Posnansky (1873 - 1946), often called "Arturo", was at various times in his life an engineer, explorer, ship's navigator, director of a river navigation company, entrepreneur, La Paz city council member, and well known and well respected a vocational archaeologist. During his lifetime, Posnansky was known as a prolific writer and researcher and for his active participation in the defence and development of Bolivia.

He was born in Austria, but at the age of 23, in 1896 moved to South America. After becoming settled down in Bolivia, Posnansky repeatedly travelled the Bolivian and Peruvian highlands in efforts to locate, describe, and study Inca and pre-Inca archaeological sites. He was especially interested in those found along the shoreline and on the islands of Lake Titicaca. The results of these investigations were published in books such as *The Islands of Titicaca and Koati* and *Rasas y monumentos prehistoricos del Altiplano Andino*.

In 1945 (volumes I and II) and 1957 (volumes III and IV), Posnansky's final and most important book, *Tihuanacu, the Cradle of American Man,* was published. In it, Posnansky argued that Tiwanaku was constructed approximately 12,000 years ago by American peoples, although not by the ancestors of those then living in the area, the Aymara. Posnansky also saw Tiwanaku as the origin point of civilization throughout the Americas, including the Inca, the Maya and others.

He was of course immediately discredited by the academics of his day, and continues to be so by conventional researchers. However, his ideas, though outlandish, are based in hard science. He was a very early user of what is now the popular tool known as archaeoastronomony to date Tiwanaku, specifically the Kalasasaya, and we shall explore this, in detail shortly, thanks to the words of Graham Hancock, in an excerpt again from his great work "Fingerprints of the Gods." I will use Graham's own account of Posnansky word for word, hopefully with his permission, since he puts the points across very clearly and succinctly, without using too much scientific jargon. As I write articles for his website: www.grahamhancock.com I don't think he will mind.

Though his dating was trashed by academics, Posnansky's ideas about the Tiwanaku Site having been full-fledged city with a large permanent population instead of having been only a seasonally occupied ceremonial center and its abandonment having been the result of prehistoric climatic change are widely accepted. Also, this book and his personal efforts contributed significantly to the eventual preservation of the Tiwanaku Site at a time when it was being very badly damaged by neglect, stone quarrying, and looting.

The basic definition of archaeoastronomy is, although we think our planet moves smoothly and evenly in a constant orbit, there are slight variations. It in fact has a slight wobble in its orbit, which is called precession, and this has a cycle of about 26,000 years. Also, another phenomenon, called obliquity of the ecliptic is the relationship of the angle of the earth's orbit in relation to the plane that it travels around the sun. This again is not fixed, and the axial tilt of the Earth oscillates between round 22.0°-24.6°, with a period of round 41,000 years.

If this sounds confusing, please look at the drawings below.

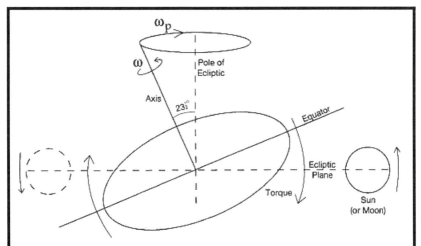

Figure 3.3. Origin of the precessional torque. The gravitational action of the Sun (and Moon) on the Earth's equatorial bulge exerts a torque that tends to pull the bulge into alignment with the instantaneous Earth-Sun (or Earth-Moon) axis. The torque vanishes when the Sun (or Moon) crosses the equatorial plane, but appears with the same sign for both halves of the orbit, causing a net average precessional torque.

Basic concept of the precession of the equinoxes cycle

The above diagram shows the wobble effect which is the basic premise of precession. Below is a drawing of how the obliquity of the ecliptic cycle works.

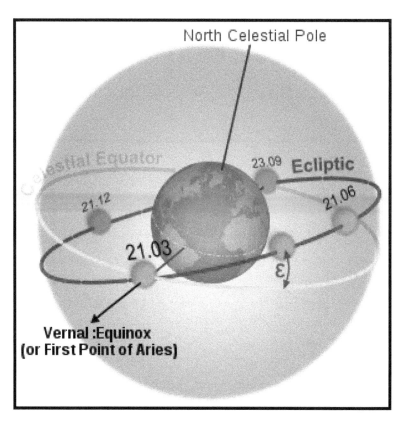

Example of the obliquity of the ecliptic process

The actual process of how these two phenomenon work is similar; any construction of importance, no matter where you find them, tends to be aligned to one of the major cardinal points, north, south, east or west, and, most cultures, through history, have been able to do this with some degree of precision. How? It is quite easy actually. The footprint, or designed placement of the temple, building etc. need be set on one of the solstices, either winter or summer. This tells the designers and builders when the sun is in direct alignment. The fact that this coincides with festivals and agricultural cycles is universal and obvious. Over the course of the millennia, the original alignment slowly goes "out of whack" and so by calculating how many parts of a degree the building is now out of alignment, one can calculate when it was built. As has been said, the precessional cycle is about 26,000 years, and the obliquity of the ecliptic 41,000 years.

Posnansky chose the obliquity to use in his calculations, and now I will let Mr. Graham Hancock tell you the rest...

"According to the dictionary definition it is 'the angle between the plane of the earth's orbit and that of the celestial equator, equal to approximately 23° 27' at present'. To clarify this obscure astronomical notion, it helps to picture the earth as a ship, sailing on the vast ocean of the heavens. Like all such vessels (be they planets or schooners), it *rolls* slightly with the swell that flows beneath it. Picture yourself on board that ship as it rolls, standing on the deck, gazing out to sea. You rise up on the crest of a wave and your visible horizon increases; you fall back into a trough and it decreases. The process is regular, mathematical, like the tick-tock of a great metronome: a constant, almost imperceptible, nodding, perpetually changing the angle between yourself and the horizon. Now picture the earth again. Floating in space, as every schoolchild knows, the axis of daily rotation of our beautiful blue planet lies slightly tilted away from the vertical in its orbit around the sun. From this it follows that the terrestrial equator, and hence the 'celestial equator' (which is merely an imaginary extension of the earth's equator into the celestial sphere) must also lie at an angle to the orbital plane. That angle at any one time, *is* the obliquity of the ecliptic. But because the earth is a ship that rolls, its obliquity *changes* in a cyclical manner over very long periods. During each cycle of 41,000 years the obliquity varies, with the precision and predictability of a Swiss chronograph, between 22.1° and 24.5°.3

The sequence in which one angle will follow another, as well as the sequence of all previous angles (at any period of history) can be calculated by means of a few straightforward equations. These have been expressed as a curve on a graph (originally plotted out in Paris in 1911 by the International Conference of Ephemerids) and from this graph it is possible to match angles and precise historical dates with confidence and accuracy. Posnansky was able to date the Kalasasaya because the obliquity cycle gradually alters the azimuth position of sunrise and sunset from century to century. By establishing the solar alignments of certain key structures that now looked 'out of true', he convincingly demonstrated that the obliquity of the ecliptic at the time of the building of the Kalasasaya had been 23° 8′ 48″. When that angle was plotted on the graph drawn up by the International Conference of Ephemerids it was found to correspond to a date of 15,000 BC.

Of course, not a single orthodox historian or archaeologist was prepared to accept such an early origin for Tiahuanaco preferring, as noted in Chapter Eight, to agree on the safe estimate of AD 500. During the years 1927-30, however, several scientists from other disciplines checked carefully Posnansky's 'astronomic-archaeological investigations'. These scientists, members of a high-powered team which also studied many other archaeological sites in the Andes, were Dr. Hans Ludendorff (then director of the Astronomical Observatory of Potsdam), Dr. Friedrich Becker of the Specula Vaticanica, and two other astronomers: Professor Dr. Arnold Kohlschutter of the University of Bonn and Dr. Rolf Muller of the Astrophysical Institute of Potsdam.

At the end of their three years of work the scientists concluded that Posnansky was basically right. They didn't concern themselves with the implications of their findings for the prevailing paradigm of history; they simply stated the observable facts about the astronomical alignments of various structures at Tiahuanaco. Of these, the most important by far was that the Kalasasaya had been laid out to conform with observations of the heavens made a very long time ago — much, much further back than AD 500. Posnansky's figure of 15,000 BC was pronounced to be well within the bounds of possibility."

Thanks again for the above to Graham, whose "Fingerprints of the Gods" is a "must read" book about the truth of the true history of earth's civilizations. As regards Puma Punku, and what could have happened to cause its utter destruction, Posnansky says this:

"This catastrophe was caused by seismic movements which resulted in an overflow of the waters of Lake Titicaca and in volcanic eruptions ... It is also possible that the temporary increase in the level of the lake may have been caused in part by the breaking of the bulwarks on some of the lakes further to the north and situated at a greater altitude ... thus releasing the waters which descended toward Lake Titicaca in onrushing and unrestrainable torrents....in chaotic disorder among wrought stones, utensils, tools and an endless variety of other things. All of this has been moved, broken and accumulated in a confused heap. Anyone who would dig a trench here two meters deep could not deny that the destructive force of water, in combination with brusque movements of the earth, must have accumulated those different kinds of bones, mixing them with pottery, jewels, tools and utensils ... Layers of alluvium cover the whole field of the ruins and lacustrine sand mixed with shells from Titicaca, decomposed feldspar and volcanic ashes have accumulated in the places surrounded by walls ..."

One of many finely shaped stones found buried at Puma Punku

Posnansky speculated that this happened about 11,000 years ago, and seems to coincide with the destructive earth changes that occurred at the end of the last Ice Age. Many theories, especially recent ones, believe that the actual melting of the great ice sheets may have happened over the course of as little as 1000 years, and the transfer of the ice into water form, and thus redistributed from solid masses near the north and south poles to being global, caused the level of the world's oceans to rise between 300 and 400 feet.

Aside from wiping any coastal dwellings and people off the map, this redistribution of weight would have been enormous pressure on the tectonic plates of the earth, causing volcanism and earthquakes of apocalyptic proportions. Again, here we have Graham Hancock's words:

"Thereafter, though the flood waters subsided, 'the culture of the Altiplano did not again attain a high point of development but fell rather into a total and definitive decadence'. This process was hastened by the fact that the earthquakes which had caused Lake Titicaca to engulf Tiahuanaco were only the first of many upheavals in the area. These initially resulted in the lake swelling and overflowing its banks but they soon began to have the opposite effect, slowly reducing Titicaca's depth and surface area. As the years passed, the lake continued to drain inch by inch, marooning the great city, remorselessly separating it from the waters which had previously played such a vital role in its economic life." The quote within the text is that of Posnansky.

This is in fact a viable hypothesis for what happened at Tiwanaku and Puma Punku. The devastation that would have resulted from such a catastrophe could very well have left the area lifeless for thousands of years. Not only would the people have been displaced, but the soil would have been lifted and carried away by the flood waters. Thus, nothing would grow. And also, going back to the oral traditions that were spoken of earlier, Viracocha is said to have destroyed a race of "giants" with a devastating flood back in deep antiquity. Perhaps these giants were not necessarily of giant size, but of huge mind.

Our tour group in November 2012 inside the excavations of Puma Punku

10/ How Tiwanaku And Puma Punku Originally Looked

As we have noted, the first Europeans to see Tiwanaku and Puma Punku, namely the Spanish soon after the conquest in1532, saw it as a destroyed place; massive well shaped stones strewn on the Altiplano like children's' toys. The sites seem not to have been heavily exploited for building materials until late in the 19th century, when the railroad was built; prior to this the movement of anything but small blocks would have been difficult, especially to distant La Paz.

The following series of photos shows us what Tiwanaku and Puma Punku looked like around 1880, and I have included modern photos to show how it looks now.

19th century drawing of, presumably, Puma Punku

Kalasasaya as photographed in the 19th century

Same entrance of the Kalasasaya as seen today

As you can see in the above two photos, the steps and solitary megaliths on either side are original; the doorway and sculpture have been added in, as have the side walls. The yellow colour on the stones is lichen; a primitive plant form that grows on stone surfaces, usually after an extended period of time. Since the lichen is on some stones and not others, this is another clue that the door/entryway stones have not been there, collectively, for longer than several decades.

One of the major red sandstone Viracocha figures

This sculpture was found approximately half buried in the ground and excavated between 1889 and 1920. The fact that it was not completely on the surface when discovered suggests, of course, that it was the victim of some sort of natural disaster, such as a flood of thick muddy water, and/or it is so ancient that sediment built up around it over time. It is presently in the new Tiwanaku museum.

Photo shows the actual size of this sculpture

Another sandstone Viracocha sculpture

The above sculpture is now on display on the grounds of Tiwanaku, and was featured earlier in this book with David Hatcher Childress. The major colouration difference between the right and left sides indicates that the left portion was most likely buried for an extended period of time, causing the right side to be more oxidized by the air and the intense sunlight of the Altiplano.

The Viracocha sculpture as seen today

Some researchers, especially those of the "ancient alien" belief system speculate that this sculpture, as well as two others are holding exotic weapons or electronic instruments in their hands. The one on the right, in the photograph, is more likely a Kero (or Qero) which is a drinking cup; this exact design was later adopted by the Inca (see below.)

Various drinking vessels found at Tiwanaku

Inca period Kero

The above cultural comparison, in this case drinking vessels, shows you that the Inca were not as inventive as they are often portrayed. They were in fact the pinnacle, and last of the great cultural expressions of the area, adopting and adapting many of the arts and sciences of other cultures.

Very early photo of Puma Punku; notice the farming to the right

Puma Punku as seen by the present day visitor

A you can see from the above two photos, taken almost 100 years apart, little work at reconstruction, or in fact anything has been done at Puma Punku, and yet, to the studious observer, it is the more intriguing of the two sites.

Precision manufactured blocks now piled like confused rubble

Why has Puma Punku received so little attention from scholars and especially the Bolivian government? Is it because so much has been removed over time that they have no idea how to piece it back together, even theoretically in diagrams? Or do the implications that the finely machined surfaces present, which could only have been achieved, as far as we know within the recent past, in fact scare them?

Andesite block from Puma Punku showing machined and
possible heat blasted surfaces

And what follows are diagrams of what some of the
Puma Punku stones would have looked like in their
original condition...

One of the famous and conspicuous "H" blocks

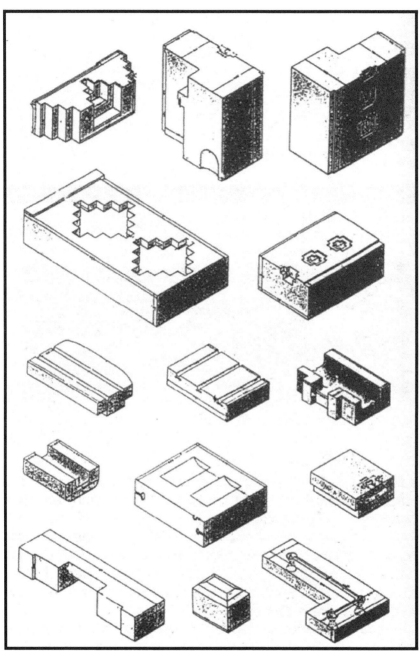

Various blocks from Puma Punku

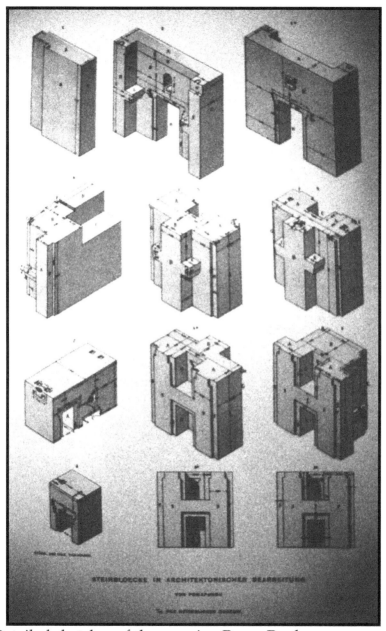

Detailed sketches of the amazing Puma Punku component stones

11/ The Early Inhabitants

And what of the people who lived there? We have seen that the Aymara have been there for about 1000 years, and that they were not the builders. Skeletons have been found in the excavations, and some are very intriguing, as they show individuals with elongated skulls.

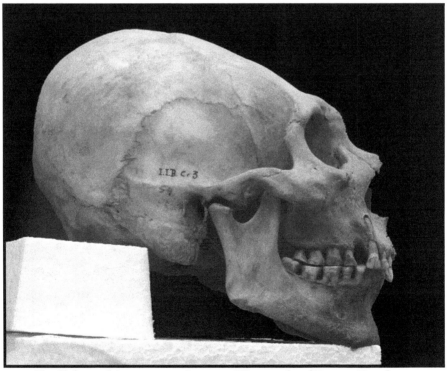

Skull found in excavations at Tiwanaku/Puma Punku

I have not been able to find out exactly from which archaeological dig the skulls have been found, whether from one or from several sites, but there clearly have been several found, as the next photo shows. Neither carbon 14 nor DNA testing of these skulls has been conducted as far as I know, so we have no idea how old they are. Also, the fact that much of the subsurface of the area, as in soil and debris has been disturbed by possible floods in the past, we have no idea how accurate archaeological digs are in terms of "deeper being older."

Display of elongated and normal skulls no longer at the Tiwanaku museum

The number of elongated skulls is by far outnumbered by those which are "normal" and so this begs the questions; who and what were the people with the elongated skulls, and were they unique to the area?

Skulls such as this have also been found on the coast of Peru, directly west of Lake Titicaca. They belong to the Paracas culture, which in fact had the largest and most elongated skulls of any human civilization that we know of; as large as 2500 cubic cm (some claim) as compared to the average modern human's 1300 cubic cm. Also, the Inca are purported to have had elongated skulls, though not as pronounced, and this phenomenon has also been documented in Egypt, Europe, the Island of Malta, Russia, Melanesia and Mexico in the past.

In the other cultures mentioned, the elongated skull was an attribute solely of the ruling and priestly classes, and this is also most likely the case with the Tiwanaku/Puma Punku skulls. In fact, since the Inca are believed to have had elongated skulls, according to a small collection in the museum of the Coricancha in Cuzco, this may in fact be a genetic trait, although no DNA comparative testing has been done as regards this as of yet.

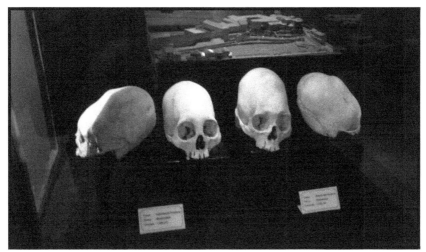

Four elongated skulls in the Coricancha museum in Cusco

Photo by D.J., a member of our November 2012 tour near Puma Punku

Another photo by D.J. from November 2012

12/ Musing Of An Early Visitor

And finally, the words of E. George Squire from his 1877 book "Peru: Incidents of Travel and Exploration in the Land of the Inca:"

'TIAHUANUCO lies almost in the very centre of the great terrestrial basin of lakes Titicaca and Aullagas, and in the heart of a region which may be properly characterized as the Tibet of the New World. Here, at an elevation of twelve thousand nine hundred feet above the sea, in a broad, open, unprotected, arid plain, cold in the wet and frigid in the dry season, we find the evidences of an ancient civilization, regarded by many as the oldest and the most advanced of both American continents.

It was to explore and investigate the monumental remains that have made this spot celebrated that I had come to Tiahuannco, and I lost no time in commencing my task. This was not an easy one, for even with the aid of the drunken *Cura* we were unable to procure laborers to assist us, for not only had we reached the village on the eve of the Chuño, or potato festival, a remnant of ancient observances, but before we had finished our work the Feast of Corpus Christi had commenced. *Chicha* flowed like water, and the few inhabitants that the Chuño festival had left sober deliberately gave themselves up to beastly intoxication.

This was not my only difficulty. While we were toiling our way upwards through the mountain road, my photographer, on whose skill I had depended, became dangerously ill. One bitter night, under an ebon sky, with no one to assist us save some kindly Indians, we tried in vain to relieve his sufferings and compose his mental hallucinations. The disease baffled all our efforts, and before sunrise death brought him relief and release. He murmured something in the Gaelic tongue, in which *only* the endearing word "mamma"—sacred in all languages—was intelligible, and died with that word lingering on his thin, blue lips. I had provided myself with a complete and costly set of photographic apparatus, which I regarded as indispensable to success in depicting the ancient monuments; but I had little knowledge of the art, and must now become my own photographer, or lose many of the results of my labor. With no instruction except such as I could gain from Hardwick's" Manual of Photographic Chemistry," I went to work, and, after numerous failures, became tolerably expert. I had but a single assistant, Mr. H-, an amateur draughtsman, and only such other aid as I could get from my muleteer and his men, who were eager to conclude their engagement, and simply astounded that we should waste an hour, much more that we should spend days, on the remains of the heathens. Still, the investigation was undertaken with equal energy and enthusiasm, and, I am confident, with as good results as could be reached without an expenditure of time and money which would hardly have been rewarded by any probable additional discoveries. We spent a week in Tiahuanuco among the ruins, and, I believe, obtained a plan of every structure that is traceable, and of every monument of importance that is extant.

The first thing that strikes the visitor in the village of Tiahuanuco is the great number of beautifully cut stones, built into the rudest edifices, and paving the squalidest courts. They are used as lintels, jambs, seats, tables, and as receptacles for water. The church is mainly built of them; the cross in front of it stands on a stone pedestal which shames the symbol it supports in excellence of workmanship. On all sides are vestiges of antiquity from the neighboring ruins, which have been a real quarry, whence have been taken the cut stones, not only for Tiahuanuco and all the villages and churches of its valley, but for erecting the cathedral of La Paz, the capital of Bolivia, situated in the deep valley of one of the streams falling into the river Beni, twenty leagues distant. And what is true here is also true of most parts of the Sierra. The monuments of the past have furnished most of the materials for the public edifices, the bridges, and highways of the present day.

The ruins of Tiahuanuco have been regarded by all students of American antiquities as in many respects the most interesting and important, and at the same time most enigmatical, of any on the continent. They have excited the admiration and wonder alike of the earliest and latest travelers, most of whom, vanquished in their attempts to penetrate the mystery of their origin, have been content to assign them an antiquity beyond that of the other monuments of America, and to regard them as the solitary remains of a civilization that disappeared before that of the Incas began, and contemporaneous with that of Egypt and the East. Unique, yet perfect in type and harmonious in style, they appear to be the work of a people who were thorough masters of an architecture which had no infancy, passed through no period of growth, and of which we find no other examples. Tradition, which mumbles more or less intelligibly of the origin of many other American monuments, is dumb concerning these. The wondering Indians told the first Spaniards that "they existed before the sun shone in the heavens," that they were raised by giants, or that they were the remains of an impious people whom an angry Deity had converted into stone because they had refused hospitality to his vice-regent and messenger.

The Kalasasaya as possibly seen from the Akapana

I shall give only a rapid account of these remains, correcting some of the errors and avoiding some of the extravagances of my predecessors in the same field of inquiry. I must confess I did not find many things that they have described; but that fact, in view of the destructiveness of treasure-hunters and the rapacity of ignorant collectors of antiquities, does not necessarily discredit their statements; for Tiahuanuco is a rifled ruin, with comparatively few yet sufficient evidences of former greatness.

The ruins are about half a mile to the southward of the village, separated from it by a small brook and a shallow valley. The high-road to La Paz passes close to them—in fact, between them and some mounds of earth which were probably parts of the general system. They are on a broad and very level part of the plain, where the soil is an arenaceous loam, firm and dry. Rows of erect stones, some of them rough or but rudely shaped by art; others accurately cut and fitted in walls of admirable workmanship; long sections of foundations, with piers and portions of stairways; blocks of stone, with mouldings, cornices, and niches cut with geometrical precision; vast masses of sandstone, trachyte, and basalt but partially hewn; and great monolithic doorways, bearing symbolical ornaments in relief, besides innumerable smaller, rectangular, and symmetrically shaped stones, rise on every hand, or lie scattered in confusion over the plain. It is only after the intelligent traveler has gone over the whole area and carefully studied the ground, that the various fragments fall into something like their just relations, and the design of the whole becomes comprehensible.

Leaving aside, for the present, the lesser mounds of earth of which I have spoken, we find the central and most conspicuous portion of the ruins, which cover not far from a square mile, to consist of a great, rectangular mound of earth, originally terraced, each terrace supported by a massive wall of cut stones, and the whole surmounted by structures of stone, parts of the foundations of which are still distinct. This structure is popularly called the" Fortress," and, as tradition affirms, suggested the plan of the great fortress of Sacsahuaman, dominating the city of Cuzco. The sides of this structure, as also of all the others in Tiahuanuco, coincide within ten degrees with the cardinal points of the compass. Close to the left of the Fortress (I adopt this name, and the others I may use, solely to facilitate description) is an area called the "Temple," slightly raised, defined by lines of erect stones, but ruder than those which surround the Fortress. A row of massive pilasters stands somewhat in advance of the eastern front of this area, and still in advance of this are the deeply embedded piers of a smaller edifice of squared stones, with traces of an exterior corridor, which has sometimes been called the "Palace." At other points, both to the south and northward, are some remains to which I shall have occasion to refer.

The structure called the Temple will claim our first attention; primarily because it seems to be the oldest of the group, the type, perhaps, of the others, and because it is here we find the great monolithic sculptured gateway of Tiahuanuco, which is absolutely unique, so far as our knowledge goes, on this continent.

The body of the Temple forms a rectangle of 388 by 445 feet, defined, as I said before, by lines of erect stones, partly shaped by art. They are mostly of red sandstone, and of irregular size and height; those at the corners being more carefully squared and tallest. For the most part, they are between 8 and 10 feet high, from 2 to 4 feet broad, and from 20 to 30 inches in thickness. The portions entering the ground, like those of our granite gateposts, are largest, and left so for the obvious purpose of giving the stones greater firmness in their position.

Early drawing of the Kalasasaya

These stones, some of which have fallen and others disappeared, seem to have been placed, inclining slightly inwards, at approximately 15 feet apart, measuring from centre to centre, and they appear to have had a wall of rough stones built up between them, supporting a *terre-plein* of earth, about 8 feet above the general level of the plain. On its eastern side this *terre-plein* had an apron or lower terrace 18 feet broad, along the edge of the central part of which were raised ten great stone pilasters, placed 15 1/2 feet apart, all of which, perfectly aligned, are still standing, with a single exception. They are of varying heights, and no two agree in width or thickness. The one that is fallen, which was second in the line, measures 13 feet 8 inches in length by 5 feet 3 inches in breadth. It is partly buried in the earth, but shows 32 inches of thickness above ground. Among those still erect the tallest is 14 feet by 4 feet 2 inches, and 2 feet 8 inches; the shortest 9 feet by 2 feet 9 inches, and 2 feet 5 inches. These are less in dimension than the stones composing the inner cell or sanctum of Stonehenge, which range from 16 feet 3 inches to 21 feet 6 inches in height; but they are nearly, if not quite, equal with those composing the outer circle of that structure. They are much more accurately cut than those of Stonehenge, the fronts being perfectly true, and the backs alone left rough or only partially worked. The tops of the taller ones have shoulders cut into them as if to receive architraves; and as this feature does not appear in the shorter ones, it may be inferred that their tops have been broken off, and that originally they were all of one length. And here I may call attention to another singular feature of this colonnade — namely, that the sides or edges of each erect stone are slightly cut away to within six inches of its face, so as to leave a projection of about an inch and a half, as if to retain in place any slab fitted between the stones, and prevent it from falling outwards. The same feature is found in the stones surrounding the great mound or Fortress, where its purpose becomes obvious, as we shall soon see.

Such is the general character of the exterior propylon, if I may so call it, of the structure called the Temple. But within the line of stones surrounding it there are other features which claim our attention. I have said that the interior is a mound of earth raised about eight feet above the general level. But in the centre and towards the western side is an area sunk to the general level, 280 feet long by 190 feet broad. It was originally defined on three sides by walls of rough stones which rose above the surface of the mound itself, but which are now in ruins. If this sunken area communicated in any way with the more elevated interior parts of the structure, the means of communication, by steps or otherwise, have disappeared. Across the end of the area not shut in by the mound, the line of stones which surrounds the Temple is continued without interruption; but outside and connected with it is part of a small square of lesser stones, also erect, standing in the open plain.

Regarding the eastern side of the Temple, marked by the line of pilasters which I have described, as the front, we find here, at the distance of 57 feet, the traces of a rectangular structure, to which I have alluded as the" Palace," which was composed of blocks of trachyte admirably cut, 8 to 10 feet long by 5 feet broad, with remains of what appears to have been a corridor 30 feet broad extending around it. The piers which supported the Palace still remain, sunk deep in the ground, apparently resting on an even pavement of cut stones. Remove the superstructures of the best-built edifices of our cities, and few, if any, would expose foundations laid with equal care, and none of them stones cut with such accuracy, or so admirably fitted together. And I may say, once for all, carefully weighing my words, that in no part of the world have I seen stones cut with such mathematical precision and admirable skill as in Peru, and in no part of Peru are there any to surpass those which are scattered over the plain of Tiahuanuco. The so-called Palace does not seem to have been placed in any symmetrical relation towards the Temple, although seemingly dependent on it; nor, in fact, do any of the ancient structures here appear to have been erected on any geometric plan respecting each other, such as is apparent in the arrangement of most of the remains of aboriginal public edifices in Peru.

Early excavation possibly at Puma Punku

The Fortress stands to the southwest of the Temple, the sides of the two coinciding in their bearings, and is 64 feet distant from it. As I have already said, it is a great mound of earth, originally rectangular in shape, 620 feet in length and 450 in width, and about 50 feet high. It is much disfigured by the operations of treasure-seekers, who have dug into its sides and made great excavations from the summit, so that it now resembles rather a huge, natural, shapeless heap of earth than a work of human hands. The few of the many stones that environed it, and which the destroyers have spared, nevertheless enable us to make out its original shape and proportions. There are distinct evidences that the body of the mound was terraced, for there are still standing stones at different elevations, distant horizontally nine, eighteen, and thirty feet from the base. There may have been more terraces than these lines of stones would indicate, but it is certain that there were at least three before reaching the summit. This coincides with what Garcilaso tells us of the mound when first visited by the Spaniards. He says, speaking of the ruins under notice: "Among them there is a mountain or hill raised by hand, which, on this account, is most admirable. In order that the piled-up earth should not be washed away and the hill leveled, it was supported by great walls of stone. No one knows for what purpose this edifice was raised." Cieza de Leon, who himself visited Tiahuanuco soon after the Conquest, gives substantially the same description of the so-called Fortress.

On the summit of this structure are sections of the foundations of rectangular buildings, partly undermined, and partly covered up by the earth from the great modern excavation in the centre, which is upwards of 300 feet in diameter, and more than 60 feet deep. A pool of water stands at its bottom. This latest piece of barbarism was, however, only in continuation of some similar previous undertaking. All over the Fortress and on its slopes lie large and regular blocks of stone, sculptured with portions of elaborate designs, which would only appear when the blocks were fitted together. Some portions of the outer or lower wall are fortunately nearly intact, so that we are able to discover how it was constructed and the plan and devices that were probably observed in all the other walls, as well as in some parts of the Temple. In the first place, large, upright stones were planted in the ground, apparently resting on stone foundations. They are about ten feet above the surface, accurately faced, perfectly aligned, and inclining slightly inwards towards the mound. They are placed seventeen feet apart from centre to centre, and are very nearly uniform in size, generally about three feet broad and two feet in thickness. Their edges are cut to present the kind of shoulders to which I alluded in describing the pilasters in front of the Temple, and of which the purpose now becomes apparent. The space between the upright stones is filled in with a wall of carefully worked stones. Those next the pilasters are cut with a shoulder to fit that of the pilaster they adjoin; and they are each, moreover, cut with alternate grooves and projections, like mortise and tenon, so as to fit immovably into each other horizontally. Vertically they are held in position by round holes drilled into the bottom and top of each stone at exact corresponding distances, in which, there is reason to believe, were placed pins of bronze. We here see the intelligent devices of a people unacquainted with the uses of cement to give strength and permanence to their structures. Nearly all the blocks of stone scattered over the plain show the cuts made to receive what is called the T clamp, and the round holes to receive the metal pins that were to retain the blocks in their places, vertically.

Detail of one of the "T" or I clamps

The Fortress has on its eastern side an apron, or dependent platform, 320 by 180 feet, of considerably less than half the elevation of the principal mound. Like the rest of the structure, its outline was defined by upright stones, most of which, however, have disappeared. The entrance seems to have been at its southeast corner, probably by steps, and to have been complicated by turnings from one terrace to another, something like those in some of the Inca fortresses.

The tradition runs that there are large vaults filled with treasure beneath the great mound, and that here commences a subterranean passage which leads to Cuzco, more than four hundred miles distant. The excavations certainly reveal some curious subterranean features. The excavation at its southwest corner has exposed a series of superimposed cut stones, apparently resting on a pavement of similar character, twelve feet below the surface. It is said that Von Tschudi, when he visited the ruins, found some "caverns" beneath them (but whether under the Fortress or not does not appear), into which he endeavored to penetrate, but "was glad to be pulled out, as he soon became suffocated." I found no such subterranean vaults or passages in any part of Tiahuanuco; but I do not deny their existence.

To the southeast of the Fortress, and about two hundred and fifty paces distant, is a long line of wall in ruins, apparently a single wall, not connected with any other so as to form an enclosure. But beyond it are the remains of edifices of which it is now impossible to form more than approximate plans. One was measurably perfect when visited by D'Orbigny in 1833, who fortunately has left a plan of it, more carefully made than others he has given us of ruins here or elsewhere. Since 1833, however, the iconoclasts have been at work with new vigor. Unable to remove the massive stones composing the base of what was called the Hall of Justice, they mined them, and blew them up with gunpowder, removing many of the elaborately cut fragments to pave the cathedral of La Paz. Enough remains to prove the accuracy of D'Orbigny's plan, and to verify what Cieza de Leon wrote concerning these particular remains three hundred years ago. The structure called the Hall of Justice occupied one end of a court something like that discoverable in the Temple. In the first place, we must imagine a rectangle, 420 feet long by 370 broad, defined by a wall of cut stones, supporting on three sides an interior platform of earth 130 feet broad, itself enclosing a sunken area, or court, also defined by a wall of cut stones. This court, which is of the general level of the plain, is 240 feet long and 160 broad. At its eastern end is, or rather was, the massive edifice distinguished' as the Hall of Justice, of which D'Orbigny says:

"It is a kind of platform of well-cut blocks of stone, held together by copper clamps, of which only the traces remain. It presents a level surface elevated six feet above the ground, 131 feet long and 23 broad, formed of enormous stones, eight making the length and two the breadth. Some of these stones are 25 1/2 feet long by 14 feet broad, and 6 1/2 feet thick. These are probably the ones measured by Oiego de Leon, who describes them as 30 feet long, 15 in width, and 6 in thickness. Some are rectangular in shape, others of irregular form. On the eastern side of the platform, and cut in the stones of which they form part, are three groups of alcoves, or seats. One group occupies the central part of the monument, covering an extent of fifty-three feet, and is divided into seven compartments. A group of three compartments occupies each extremity of the monument. Between the central and side groups were reared monolithic doorways, similar in some respects to the large one, only simpler, the one to the west alone having a sculptured frieze similar to that of the great gateway. In front of this structure, to the west, and about twenty feet distant, is a wall remarkable for the fine cutting of its stones, which are of blackish basalt and very hard. The stones arc all of equal dimensions, having a groove running around them, and each has a niche cut in it with absolute precision. Everything goes to show that the variety of the forms of the niches was one of the great ornaments of the walls, for on all sides we find stones variously cut, and evidently intended to fit together so as to form architectural ornaments." So much for the description of D'Orbigny. I measured one of the blocks with a double niche, which is shown in the engraving of the terrace walls of the Fortress. It is 6 feet 2 inches in length, 3 feet 7 inches broad, and 2 feet 6 inches thick. The niches are sunk to the depth of 3 inches. One of the monolithic doorways originally belonging to this structure is unquestionably that forming the entrance to the cemetery of Tiahuanuco. This cemetery is an ancient rectangular mound, about a hundred paces long, sixty broad, and twenty feet high, situated midway between the village and the Fortress. Its summit is enclosed by an adobe wall, and, as I have said, the entrance is through an ancient monolithic gateway, of which I give a front and rear view. It is 7 feet 5 inches in extreme height, 5 feet 10 1/2 inches in extreme width, and 16 1/2 inches thick. The doorway, or opening, is 6 feet 2 inches in height, and 2 feet 10 inches wide. The frieze has a repetition of the ornaments composing the lower line of sculptures of the great monolith, but it has suffered much from time and violence. The ornamentation of the back differs from that of the front, and seems to have been made to conform to the style adopted in the interior of the structure. In making our measurement in the cemetery we disturbed a pack of lean, hungry, savage dogs of the Sierra-an indigenous species—which had dug up the body of a newly-buried child from its shallow, frozen grave, and were ravenously devouring it. They snarled at us with bristling backs and bloodshot eyes as we endeavored to drive them away horn their horrible feast—by no means the first, as the numerous rough holes they had dug, the torn wrappings of the dead, and the skulls and fragments of human bodies scattered around too plainly attested. I subsequently represented the matter to the *cura,* but he only shrugged his shoulders, ejaculating, "What does it matter? They have been baptized, and all Indians are brutes at the best."

Returning to the Hall of Justice, we find, to the eastward of it, a raised area 175 feet square, and from 8 to 10 feet high, the outlines defined by walls of cut stone. This seems to have escaped the notice of travelers; at least, it is not mentioned by them. In the centre of this area there seems to have been a building about fifty feet square, constructed of very large blocks of stone, which I have denominated the" Sanctuary." Within this, where it was evidently supported on piers, is the distinctive and most remarkable feature of the structure. It is a great slab of stone 13 feet 4 inches square, and 20 inches in thickness. It is impossible to describe it intelligibly, and I must refer to the engraving for a notion of its character. It will be observed that there is an oblong area cut in the upper face of the stone, 7 feet 3 inches long, 5 feet broad, and 6 inches deep. A sort of sunken "portico" 20 inches wide, 3 feet 9 inches long, is cut at one side, out of which opens what may be called the entrance, 22 inches wide, extending to the edge of the stone.

Astonishing stone work buried at Puma Punku

At each end of the "portico" is a flight of three miniature steps leading up to the general surface of the stone, and sunk in it, while at the side of the excavated area are three other flights of similar steps, but in relief. They lead to the broadest part of the stone, where there are six mortises, 8 inches square, sunk in the stone. 6 inches, and forming two sides of a square, of 3 feet 7 inches on each side, and apparently intended to receive an equal number of square columns. The external corners of the stone are sharp, but within six inches of the surface they are cut round on a radius of twelve inches. I cannot resist the impression that this stone was intended as a miniature representation or model of a sacred edifice, or of some kind of edifice reared by the builders of the monuments of Tiahuanuco. The entrance to the sunken area in the stone, the steps leading to the elevation surrounding it, and the *naos* opposite the entrance, defined perhaps by columns of bronze or stone set in the mortises and supporting some kind of roof, constituting the shrine within which stood the idol or symbol of worship—all these features would seem to indicate a symbolic design in this monument. The building in which it stood, on massive piers that still remain, was constructed of blocks of stone, some of them nearly fourteen feet in length and of corresponding size and thickness, and was not so large as to prohibit the probability that it was covered in. Looking at the plan of the Temple, and of the enclosure to the area, one side of which was occupied by the building called the Hall of Justice, we cannot fail to observe features suggestive of the plan cut in the great stone which I have called symbolical. The most remarkable monument in Tiahuanuco, as already intimated, is the great monolithic gateway. Its position is indicated by the letter *m* in the plan. It now stands erect, and is described as being in that position by every traveler except D'Orbigny, who visited the ruins in 1833, and who says it had then fallen down. I give two views of this unique monument, both from photographs, of some interest to me, as the first it was ever my fortune to be called on to take. It will be seen that it has been broken—the natives say by lightning—the fracture extending from the upper right-hand angle of the opening, so that the two parts lap by each other slightly, making the sides of the doorway incline towards each other; whereas they are, or were, perfectly. vertical and parallel—a distinguishing side two small niches, below which, also on either side, is a single larger niche. The stone itself is a dark and exceedingly hard trachyte. It is faced with a precision that no skill can excel; its lines are perfectly drawn, and its right angles turned with an accuracy that the most careful geometer could not surpass. Barring some injuries and defacements, and some slight damages by weather, I do not believe there exists a better piece of stone-cutting, the material considered, on this or the other continent. The front, especially the part covered by sculpture, has a fine finish, as near a true polish as trachyte can be made to bear.

Detail of the Gateway of the Sun

The lower line of sculpture is 7 1/2 inches broad, and is unbroken; the three above it are 8 inches high, cut up in *cartouches,* or squares, of equal width, but interrupted in the centre, immediately over the doorway, by the figure in high-relief to which I have alluded. This figure, with its ornaments, covers a space of 32 by 21 1/2 inches. There are consequently three ranges or tiers of squares on each side of this figure, eight in each range, or forty-eight in all. The figures represented in these squares have human bodies, feet, and hands; each holds a sceptre; they are winged; but the upper and lower series have human heads wearing crowns, represented in profile, while the heads of the sixteen figures in the line between them have the heads of condors.

The central and principal figure is angularly but boldly cut, in a style palpably conventional. The head is surrounded by a series of what may be called rays, each terminating in a circle, the head of the condor, or that of a tiger, all conventionally but forcibly treated. In each hand he grasps two staves or sceptres of equal length with his body, the lower end of the right-hand sceptre terminating in the head of the condor, and the upper in that of the tiger, while the lower end of the left-hand sceptre terminates in the head of the tiger, and the upper is bifurcate, and has two heads of the condor. The staves or sceptres are not straight and stiff, but curved as if to represent serpents, and elaborately ornamented as if to represent the sinuous action of the serpent in motion. The radiations from the head — which I have called rays, for want of a better term — seem to have the same action. An ornamented girdle surrounds the waist of this principal figure, from which depends a double fringe. It stands upon a kind of base or series of figures approaching nearest in character to the architectural ornament called *grecques,* each extremity of which, however, terminates in the crowned head of the tiger or the condor. The face has been somewhat mutilated, but shows some peculiar figures extending from the eyes diagonally across the cheeks, terminating also in the heads of the animals just named.

The winged human-headed and condor-headed figures in the three lines of squares are represented kneeling on one knee, with their faces turned to the great central figure, as if in adoration, and each one holds before him a staff or sceptre. The sceptres of the figures in the two upper rows are bifurcate, and correspond exactly with the sceptre in the left hand of the central figure, while the sceptres of the lower tier correspond with that represented in his right hand. The relief of all these figures is scarcely more than two-tenths of an inch; the minor features are indicated by very delicate lines, slightly incised, which form subordinate figures, representing the heads of condors, tigers, and serpents. Most of us have seen pictures and portraits of men and animals, which under close attention resolve themselves into representatives of a hundred other things, but which are so artfully arranged as to produce a single broad effect. So with these winged figures. Every part, the limbs, the garb, all separate themselves into miniatures of the symbols that run all through the sculptures on this singular monument. The fourth or lower row of sculpture differs entirely from the rows above it. It consists of repetitions — seventeen in all — smaller and in low-relief, of the head of the great central figure, surrounded by corresponding rays, terminating in like manner with the heads of animals. These are arranged alternately at the top and bottom of the line of sculpture, within the zigzags or *grecques,* and every angle terminates in the head of a condor.

The three outer columns of winged figures, and the corresponding parts of the lower line of sculpture, are only blocked out, and have none of the elaborate, incised ornamentation discoverable in the central parts of the monument. A very distinct line separates these unfinished sculptures from those portions that are finished, which is most marked in the lower tier. On each side of this line, standing on the rayed heads to which I have alluded, placed back to back, and looking in opposite directions, are two small but interesting figures of men, crowned with something like a plumed cap, and holding to their mouths what appear to be trumpets. Although only three inches high, these little figures are ornamented in the same manner as the larger ones, with the heads of tigers, condors, etc. These are the only sculptures on the face of the great monolith of Tiahuanuco. I shall not attempt to explain their significance. D'Orbigny finds in the winged figures with human heads symbols or representations of conquered chiefs coming to pay their homage to the ruler who had his capital in Tiahuanuco, and who, as the founder of sun-worship and the head of the Church as of the State, was invested with divine attributes as well as with the insignia of power. The figures with condors' heads, the same fanciful philosopher supposes, may represent the chiefs of tribes who had not yet fully accepted civilization, and were therefore represented without the human profile, as an indication of their unhappy and undeveloped state. By parity of interpretation, we may take it that the eighteen unfinished figures were those of as many chieftains as the ruler of Tiahuanuco had it in his mind to reduce, and of which, happily, just two-thirds had claims to be regarded as civilized, and, when absorbed, to be perpetuated with human heads, and not with those of condors. Another French writer, M. Angrand, finds a coincidence between these sculptures and those of Central America and Mexico, having a corresponding mythological and symbolical significance, thus establishing identity of origin and intimate relationship between the builders of Tiahuanuco and those of Palenque, Ocosingo, and Xochicalco. Leibnitz tells us that nothing exists without a cause; and it is not to be supposed that the sculptures under notice were made without a motive. They are probably symbolical; but with no knowledge of the religious ideas and conceptions of the ancient people whose remains they are, it is idle to attempt to interpret them. Nowhere else in Peru, or within the whole extent of the Inca Empire, do we find any similar sculptures. They are, as regards Inca art, quite as unique in Peru as they would be on Boston Common or in the New York Central Park. The reverse of the great monolith shows a series of friezes over the doorway, five in number, of which the engraving will give a better idea than any description. Above the entrance on either hand are two niches, twelve by nine inches in the excavation. It will be observed that those on the right have a sort of sculptured cornice above them which those on the left have not. The second one on the left, it will also be observed, is not complete, but evidently intended to be finished out on another block, which was to form a continuation of the wall of which the gateway itself was designed to be a part. Indeed, as I have said, nearly all the blocks of stone scattered over the plain are cut with parts of niches and other architectural features, showing that they were mere fragments of a general design, which could only be clearly apparent when they were properly fitted together.

The lower niches, now on a level with the ground, show that the monolith is sunk deeply in the soil. They exhibit some peculiar features. At each inner corner above and below are vertical sockets, apparently to receive the pivots of a door, extending upwards and downwards seven inches in the stone. D'Orbigny avers that he discovered the stains of bronze in these orifices and I have no doubt that these niches had doors, possibly of bronze, hinged in these sockets, and so firmly that it was necessary to use chisels (the marks of which are plain) to cut into the stone and disengage them. These large niches are 28.2 inches by 18.2 inches wide. On the face of the monolith, on each side of the doorway, but near the edges of the stone, are two mortises 10 inches by 9, and 6 inches deep, and 12 inches by 6, and 3 1/2 inches deep respectively, which are not shown in the drawings published by D'Orbigny and some others.

I very much question if this remarkable stone occupies its original position. How far it has sunk in the ground it was impossible for me to determine, for the earth was frozen hard, and we had no means of digging down to ascertain. D'Orbigny, as I have already said, states it was fallen when he visited it. Who has since raised it, and for what purpose, it is impossible to say. No one that we could find either knew or cared to know anything about it. It seems to me not unlikely that it had a position in the hollow square of the structure called the Temple, in some building corresponding with that called the Hall of Justice. Or, perhaps, it had a place in the structure enclosing the stone I have ventured to call symbolical. It is neither so large nor so heavy that it may not be moved by fifty men with ropes, levers, and rollers and although we know not know of any reason why it should have been removed from its original position, we know that many of the heaviest stones have been thus moved, including the monolithic doorway at the entrance of the cemetery. In addition to the various features of Tiahuanuco already enumerated, I must not neglect to notice the vast blocks of unhewn and partially hewn stones that evidently have never entered into any structure, which lie scattered among the ruins. The positions of two or three are indicated in the plan. The one to the northeast of the Temple is 26 by 17, and 3 1/2 feet aboveground. It is of red sandstone, with deep grooves crossing each other at right angles in the centre, twenty inches deep, as if an attempt had been made to cut the stone into four equal parts. Another of nearly equal dimensions, partly hewn, was between the Temple and the Fortress. Another, boat-shaped and curiously grooved, lies to the northwest of the great mound. It measures upwards of forty feet in length, and bears the marks of transportation from a considerable distance.

There were formerly a number of specimens of sculpture in Tiahuanuco besides the two monolithic gateways I have described. Says Oiego de Leon: "Beyond this hill [referring to the Fortress] are two stone idols, of human shape, and so curiously carved that they seem to be the work of very able masters. They are as big as giants, with long garments differing from those the natives wear, and seem to have some ornament on their heads." These, according to D'Orbigny, were broken into pieces by blasts of powder inserted between the shoulders, and not even the fragments remain on the plain of Tiahuanuco. The head of one lies by the side of the road, four leagues distant, on the way to La Paz, whither an attempt was made to carry it. I did not see it, but I reproduce the sketch of it given by D'Orbigny, merely remarking that I have no doubt the details are quite as erroneous as those of the figures portrayed by the same author on the great monolith. The head is 3 feet 6 inches high and 2 feet 7 inches in diameter; so that if the other proportions of the figure were corresponding, the total height of the statue would be about eighteen feet.

D'Orbigny found several other sculptured figures among the ruins; one with a human head and wings rudely represented; another of an animal resembling a tiger, etc. Castelnau mentions "an immense lizard cut in stone," and other sculptured figures. M. Angrand, whose notes have been very judiciously used by M. Desjardains, speaks of eight such figures in the village of Tiahuanuco, besides two in La Paz, and one, broken, on the road thither. I found but two; rough sculptures of the human head and bust, in coarse red sandstone, one of a man and the other of a woman, standing by the side of the gateway of the church of Tiahuanuco. They are between four and five feet high, roughly cut, much defaced, and more like the idols which I found in Nicaragua, and have represented in my work on that country, than any others I have seen elsewhere.

Three Viracocha style figures found at Tiwanaku

Among the stones taken from the ruins, and worked into buildings in the town of Tiahuanuco, are a number of cylindrical columns cut from a single block, with capitals resembling the Doric. One of these stands on each side of the entrance to the court of the church, 6 feet high and 14 inches in diameter. There are also many caps of square columns or pilasters, besides numbers of stones cut with deep single or double grooves, as if to serve for water-conduits when fitted together — a purpose the probability of which is sanctioned by finding some stones with channels leading off at right angles, like the elbows in our own water-pipes.

The stones composing the structures of Tiahuanuco, as already said, are mainly red sandstone, slate-colored trachyte, and a dark, hard basalt. None of these rocks are found *in situ* on the plain, but there has been much needless speculation as to whence they were obtained. There are great cliffs of red sandstone about five leagues to the north of the ruins, on the road to the Desaguadero; and, on the isthmus of Yunguyo, connecting the peninsula of Copacabana with the mainland, are found both basaltic and trachytic rocks, identical with the stones in the ruins. Many blocks, hewn or partially hewn, are scattered over the isthmus. It is true this point is forty miles distant from Tiahuanuco in a right line, and that, if obtained here; the stones must have been carried twenty-five miles by water and fifteen by land. That some of them were brought from this direction is indicated by scattered blocks all the way from the ruins to the lake; but it is difficult to conceive how they were transported from one shore to the other. There is no timber in the region of which to construct rafts or boats; and the only contrivances for navigation are floats, made of reeds, closely bound into cylinders, tapering at the ends, which are turned up so as to give them something of the outline of boats. Before they become water-soaked these floats are exceedingly light and buoyant.

As to how the stones of Tiahuanuco were cut, and with what kind of instruments, are questions which I do not propose to discuss. I may, nevertheless, observe that I have no reason to believe that the builders of Tiahuanuco had instruments differing essentially in form or material from those used by the Peruvians generally, which, it is certain, were of *champi,* a kind of bronze.

Astonishing flatness of the Puma Punku work

I have thus rapidly presented an outline of the remains of Tiahuanuco-remains most interesting, but in such an absolute condition of ruin as almost to defy inquiry or generalization. Regarding them as in some respects the most important of any in Peru, I have gone more into details concerning them than I shall do in describing the better-preserved and more intelligible monuments with which we shall have hereafter to deal.

We find on a review that, apart from five considerable mounds of earth now shapeless, with one exception, there are distinct and impressive traces of five structures, built of stones or defined by them—the Fortress, the Temple, the Palace, the Hall of Justice, and the Sanctuary—terms used more to distinguish than truly characterize them. The structure called the Fortress may indeed have been used for the purpose implied in the name. Terraced, and each terrace faced with stones, it may have been, as many of the terraced pyramids of Mexico were, equally temple and fortress, where the special protection of the divinity to whom it was reared was expected to be interposed against an enemy. But the absence of water and the circumscribed area of the structure seem to weigh against the supposition of a defensive origin or purpose. But, whatever its object, the Fortress dominated the plain; and when the edifices that crowned its summit were perfect, it must have been by far the most imposing structure in Tiahuanuco.

The Temple seems to me to be the most ancient of all the distinctive monuments of Tiahuanuco. It is the American Stonehenge. The stones defining it are rough and frayed by time. The walls between its rude pilasters were of uncut stones; and although it contains the most elaborate single monument among the ruins, and notwithstanding the erect stones constituting its portal are the most striking of their kind, it nevertheless has palpable signs of age, and an air of antiquity which we discover in none of its kindred monuments. Of course, its broad area was never roofed in, whatever may have been the case with smaller, interior buildings no longer traceable. We must rank it, therefore, with those vast open temples (for of its sacred purpose we can scarcely have a doubt), of which Stonehenge and Avebury, in England, are examples, and which we find in Brittany, in Denmark, in Assyria, and on the steppes of Tartary, as well as in the Mississippi Valley. It seems to me to have been the nucleus around which the remaining monuments of Tiahuanuco sprung up, and the model upon which some of them were fashioned. How far, in shape or arrangement, it may have been symbolical, I shall not undertake to say; but I think that students of antiquity are generally prepared to concede a symbolical significance to the primitive pagan temples as well as to the cruciform edifices of Christian times.

We can hardly conceive of remains so extensive as those of Tiahuanuco, except as indications of a large population, and as evidences of the previous existence on or near the spot of a considerable city. But we find nowhere in the vicinity any decided traces of ancient habitations, such as abound elsewhere in Peru, in connection with most public edifices. Again, the region around is cold, and for the most part arid and barren. Elevated nearly thirteen thousand feet above the sea, no cereals grow except barley, which often fails to mature, and seldom, if ever, so perfects itself as to be available for seed. The maize is dwarf and scant, and uncertain in yield; and the bitter potato and quinoa constitute almost the sole articles of food for the pinched and impoverished inhabitants. This is not, *prima facie*, a region for nurturing or sustaining a large population, and certainly not one wherein we should expect to find a capital. Tiahuanuco may have been a sacred spot or shrine, the position of which was determined by an accident, an augury, or a dream, but I can hardly believe that it was a seat of dominion. Some vague traditions point to Tiahuanuco as the spot whence Manco Capac, the founder of the Inca dynasty, took his origin, and whence he started northwards to teach the rude tribes of the Sierra religion and government; and some late writers, D'Orbigny and Castelnau among them, find reasons for believing that the whole Inca civilization originated here, or was only a reflex of that which found here a development, never afterwards equaled, long before the golden staff of the first Inca sunk into the earth where Cuzco was founded, thus fixing through superhuman design the site of the imperial city. But the weight of tradition points to the rocky islands of Lake Titicaca as the cradle of the Incas, whence Manco Capac and Mama Ocllo, his wife and sister, under the behest of their father, the Sun, started forth on their beneficent mission. Certain it is that this lake and its islands were esteemed sacred, and that on the latter were reared structures, if not so imposing as many other and perhaps later ones, yet of peculiar sanctity.'

Skeleton of Elongated Skull child found in the area

And with that, I leave you, the reader, to explore these enigmatic remains at your leisure, or, if you don't plan to, or even can't visit here, to leave this book hopefully somewhat wiser as to one of the most mysterious places on the planet. This is by no means the most thorough treatise ever written about Tiwanaku and Puma Punku, but is meant as an introduction.

For a deeper look into the subject, I suggest my book "Lost Ancient Technology of Peru And Bolivia" which is available below.

Brien Foerster

Cusco 2013

13/ Bibliography

(1) Fagan, Brian M. *The Seventy Great Mysteries of the Ancient World: Unlocking the Secrets of Past Civilizations*. New York: Thames & Hudson, 2001.

(2) Kolata, Alan L. (December 15, 1993). *The Tiwanaku: Portrait of an Andean Civilization*. Wiley-Blackwell. ISBN 978-1557861832.

(3) Vranich, A., 1999, *Interpreting the Meaning of Ritual Spaces: The Temple Complex of Pumapunku, Tiwanaku, Bolivia*. Doctoral Dissertation, The University of Pennsylvania.

(4) Vranich, A., 1999, *Interpreting the Meaning of Ritual Spaces: The Temple Complex of Pumapunku, Tiwanaku, Bolivia*. Doctoral Dissertation, The University of Pennsylvania.

(5) Vranich, A., 1999, *Interpreting the Meaning of Ritual Spaces: The Temple Complex of Pumapunku, Tiwanaku, Bolivia*. Doctoral Dissertation, The University of Pennsylvania.

(6) Morell, Virginia (2002). *Empires Across the Andes* National Geographic. Vol. 201, Iss. 6: 106

(7) McAndrews, Timothy L. et al. 'Regional Settlement Patterns in the Tiwanaku Valley of Bolivia'. *Journal of Field Archaeology* 24 (1997): 67-83.

(8) Blom, Deborah E. and John W. Janusek. 'Making Place: Humans as Dedications in Tiwanaku'. *World Archaeology* (2004): 123-141.

(9) Kolata, Alan L. *Valley of the Spirits: A Journey into the Lost Realm of the Aymara.* John Wiley and Sons, Hoboken, 1996.

(10)   Kolata, Alan L. (December 15, 1993). *The Tiwanaku: Portrait of an Andean Civilization.* Wiley-Blackwell. ISBN 978-1557861832.

(11)Lechtman, Heather N., MacFarlane, and Andrew W., 2005, "La metalurgia del bronce en los Andes Sur Centrales: Tiwanaku y San Pedro de Atacama". *Estudios Atacameños*, vol. 30, pp. 7-27.

(11)   Ponce Sanginés, C. and G. M. Terrazas, 1970, *Acerca De La Procedencia Del Material Lítico De Los Monumentos De Tiwanaku.* Publication no. 21. Academia Nacional de Ciencias de Bolivia

(12)   Stone-Miller, Rebecca (1995 and 2002). *Art of the Andes: from Chavin to Inca.*

(13)   Bray, Tamara L. *The Archaeology and Politics of Food and Feasting in Early States and Empires*. New York: Kluwer Academic/Plenum Publishers, 2003

(14)   Rodman, Amy Oakland (1992). *Textiles and Ethnicity: Tiwanaku in San Pedro de Atacama.*

(15)   Kolata, Alan L. (December 15, 1993). *The Tiwanaku: Portrait of an Andean Civilization.* Wiley-Blackwell. ISBN 978-1557861832. Retrieved 9 August 2009.

(16)   Protzen, J.-P., and S. E. Nair, 2000, "On Reconstructing Tiwanaku Architecture": *The Journal of the Society of Architectural Historians.* vol. 59, no., 3, pp. 358-371.

(17)   anonymous, 2005, *Harvard Summer Program in Tiwanaku, Bolivia.* Harvard Summer School Archives, Harvard University.

(18)   Isbell, W. H., 2004, *Palaces and Politics in the Andean Middle Horizon.* in S. T. Evans and J. Pillsbury, eds., pp. 191-246. *Palaces of the Ancient New World.* Dumbarton Oaks Research Library and Collection Washington, D.C.

(19)   Browman, D. L. (1981) "New light on Andean Tiwanaku". New Scientist. vol. 69, no. 4, pp. 408-419.